The Transformative Years

of the

University of Alabama Law School

ALSO BY
DANIEL JOHN MEADOR

NONFICTION

Preludes to Gideon (1967)

Criminal Appeals—English Practices and American Reforms (1973)

Mr. Justice Black and His Books (1974)

Appellate Courts—Staff and Process in the Crisis of Volume (1974)

Justice on Appeal (with P. Carrington and M. Rosenberg; 1976)

Impressions of Law in East Germany (1986)

Appellate Courts in the United States (2d ed., 2006)

American Courts (3d ed., with G. Mitchell; 2009)

FICTION

His Father's House (1994)

Unforgotten (1998)

Remberton (2007)

The
Transformative Years
of the
University of Alabama
Law School, 1966–1970

Daniel John Meador

Foreword by Judge Truman Hobbs

NewSouth Books
Montgomery

NewSouth Books
105 S. Court Street
Montgomery, AL 36104

Library of Congress Cataloging-in-Publication Data

Meador, Daniel John.
Transformative years of the University of Alabama Law School, 1966–1970
/ Daniel John Meador.

p. cm.

ISBN 13: 978 1 60306-152-0 (hardcover)
ISBN-10: 1-60306-152-5 (hardcover)
ISBN-13: 978-1-60306-153-7 (ebook)
ISBN-10: 1-60306-153-3 (ebook)

1. University of Alabama. School of Law—History—20th century.
2. Law schools—Alabama—Tuscaloosa—History—20th century.
3. Meador, Daniel John. 4. Deans (Education)—Alabama—Tuscaloosa.
I. Title.
KF292.A514M43 2012
340.071'176184—dc23

2011052270

Design by Randall Williams
Printed in the United States of America

To the memory of Jan,
who sustained me through it all
and graciously served as
unofficial Law School hostess

CONTENTS

FOREWORD

TRUMAN HOBBS
United States District Judge

In the summer of 1965, Dr. Frank Rose, president of the University of Alabama, decided that the University of Alabama Law School needed a dean to advance it further along the road of academic excellence. He contacted a young native Alabamian, Dan Meador, a graduate of the University of Alabama's Law School. Meador in 1965 was a professor at the University of Virginia Law School. Dr. Rose requested that Professor Meador come back to head his home-state law school as its dean. Meador accepted the call—pending completion of a Fulbright Lectureship in England—and more than forty years later he has written this book describing the vision he had as the new dean and the success he had in implementing that vision in the four years that he served.

He knew that success in achieving the vision could not be possible by a dean acting alone. The book describes his efforts and success in enlisting a number of able graduates, faculty, and friends of the law school to join in the vision for an even better law school. The new dean chose well in those whom he asked to serve. Many were busy lawyers in the state of Alabama, and the hard work they undertook was a credit to them and was vital to achieving the new vision for the law school.

Dean Meador had the requisite background for the task he was assuming. He held degrees from Auburn University, the University of Alabama Law School, and Harvard University. He had served as a law clerk to a distinguished University of Alabama Law School graduate, Supreme Court Justice Hugo L. Black. He was chairman of the Southeastern Conference of American Law Schools and had served on American Bar Association accreditation committees to evaluate the law schools at Duke and Vanderbilt.

Meador took as his challenge the moving of the Alabama Law School to a higher level of quality in every respect. This challenge required securing substantial funding beyond state appropriations, which required enlisting the busy lawyers mentioned above, who also wanted the best for the Alabama Law School. The state of Alabama, and the South generally, had not previously established a strong tradition of charitable giving by its attorneys. There was a generally accepted view that a state law school should be supported by state funds. But more and more state schools were finding that state funds alone were inadequate to provide the improvements that were wanted if a state law school was to achieve the desired level of excellence. In Meador's first year as dean of the Alabama Law School, he increased contributions from private sources by more than sevenfold. Dr. Rose also fulfilled his promises and the University increased the funding that it provided to the law school by almost a third.

Great progress was made at the University of Alabama Law School in the four years that Dan Meador was its dean. President Rose was pleased with the progress and was very supportive of Meador's vision, but in 1969 he resigned as president of the University.

Soon after, Dean Meador was asked if he would return to the Virginia Law School to take over the James Monroe Professorship. He had always expected someday to return to being a full-time law professor, which had more personal appeal to him than the administrative responsibilities of a dean.

Dr. Rose had been beneficial in effecting the changes made under Meador's deanship, but Meador felt that the new president was backing off from these commitments. It was difficult to understand why several of the faculty at the law school and the new president of the University of Alabama did not share Meador's enthusiasm for the changes that had been initiated, leaving him with concerns that the improvements at the law school would not be sustained. He accepted the prestigious professorship at the University of Virginia Law School and returned to the classroom.

Meador was wrong, however, in fearing that the improvements at the University of Alabama Law School would unravel under a different president; most of the achievements of Dean Meador and those who worked with him to fulfill his vision for the law school appear to be firmly in place, evidence of the skill and craftsmanship of those who worked to accomplish these goals. This book reveals the blueprint for the efforts that achieved so much for the law school during four short years.

PREFACE

The School of Law at the University of Alabama in the early twenty-first century has its roots in the late 1960s. In that time, seeds were sown and ideas and programs implanted that have grown and developed in the decades since. Many—perhaps most—of the important features of the School as it now is can be traced to the years 1966–70. Those years mark the transition from the School of the past to the School of the future. They were transformative and represent the founding period for the modern Law School. The pages that follow present an eyewitness account of those years.

They were heady years, exciting and frustrating, with much happening on all fronts. What was accomplished was not done easily. It is unlikely that I recall all the details—after all, it has been forty years—and I will be happy to be corrected if further research or other accounts reveal inaccuracies. In the meantime, this is how I see that time from the vantage point of four decades later.

The published sources for this account are the annual Law School catalogs,[1] the annual reports of the Law School Foundation,[2] and numerous issues of the student newspaper.[3] Additional sources are unpublished memoranda, committee reports, Dean's annual reports, and the like.[4] Those sources are supplemented by my memory from serving through those years as the School's dean. Indeed, my memory is the sole source for some of the facts and observations contained here.

TIME, NOT SURPRISINGLY, has taken its toll after more than forty years. The ranks of those who served on the faculty during my deanship have greatly thinned. The law alumni with whom I worked most closely are now all gone. The upshot is that living witnesses with firsthand knowledge of the events recounted here, and who might have assisted in my recollections, are few.

Four who did serve on the faculty during that time and who generously undertook to read the manuscript are Wythe W. Holt Jr., Julian B. McDonnell Jr., W. Taylor Reveley III, and L. Vastine Stabler Jr. Also, Fournier J. (Boots) Gale III, a member of the Law Class of 1969, devoted time to reading the manuscript. In the years since, all in different ways have had outstanding legal careers. They made helpful comments and suggestions and refreshed my memory on some points. They helped me relive those long-ago Farrah Hall days. I am most grateful to them. However, I alone am responsible for what is said here.

I express my appreciation to Mary Ketcham and Catherine Lamb, my office assistants, for their essential help in editing and in preparing the manuscript for publication.

1   University of Alabama Law School Catalogues for 1967, 1968, 1969, and 1970.
2   University of Alabama Law School Foundation Reports 1967, 1968, and 1969.
3   The *Alabama Law Reporter* Vol. I No. I – Vol. III No. I (1967-69).
4   Unpublished items, or copies thereof, are in possession of the author.

THE TRANSFORMATIVE YEARS
OF THE
UNIVERSITY OF ALABAMA LAW SCHOOL

1

BACKGROUND

In the late summer of 1965, I received a telephone call from Dr. Frank Rose, president of the University of Alabama. He informed me that M. Leigh Harrison would be retiring as dean of the law school the following year. He wondered whether I would be interested in the position. This call was so surprising that I hardly knew what to say. At that time I was on the law faculty at the University of Virginia and not at all anxious to leave. Moreover, my situation was complicated in that I would shortly depart for England with my wife and three children to spend a year as a Fulbright Lecturer. Nevertheless, we agreed to meet in Washington to explore the idea.

At the Mayflower Hotel, we had a lengthy and wide-ranging discussion about the school. What sticks most clearly in my mind is his statement that he intended "to do for the law school what I did for the medical school." I was familiar with what had been happening at the University of Alabama Medical School in Birmingham in recent years because my brother was on the faculty there. With huge increases in funding and able, progressive leadership, that school had been brought to national recognition. So Dr. Rose's statement carried a powerful message. If he intended to do the same for the law school, all sorts of possibilities were opened up. He held before me that exciting prospect.

In addition, this was not an offer of just any law school deanship. The University of Alabama was my alma mater. It was home. My roots ran deep in the state, and I had an abiding concern over its future. Also, I was a member of the law school class of 1951, and the opportunity to return as dean was especially attractive. Given all that, along with Frank Rose's commitments of support, it was probably a foregone conclusion that I would accept the position.

My decision was influenced to an extent by what was happening at the University of Georgia Law School. In January 1964, I had been offered the deanship there. A group of its alumni from major Atlanta law firms had determined to build up their school. They were committed to raising large amounts of money to create endowed professorships, enlarge the library, and add significantly to the building. As one put it, "Harvard would become the Georgia of the North." Governor Carl Sanders joined the effort and invited me to breakfast at the governor's mansion to exert maximum persuasion. It was an exciting prospect. In the Deep South for the first time here was an unprecedented effort to pull the region out of its long back seat in legal education and to train a new generation of enlightened leaders. It was tempting. But in the end I turned it down, as I had no ambition to be a dean. I thought that at the University of Virginia I already had one of the finest positions in legal education. At the same time, I had a twinge of guilt over failing to answer this call from my native region. Then along came Alabama, and that was different. To have turned down the deanship there would, I thought, have been to shirk my duty to my home state. There would have been a greater, lasting sense of guilt, more than what I had felt in declining the Georgia opportunity.

The relevance of the Georgia offer is that I thought that if an all-out effort for the state law school was being mounted in Georgia, then a similar development should be possible in Alabama. In my view, success would depend heavily on whether the Alabama law alumni could be motivated like those Atlanta lawyers to provide substantial financial support for their school—something the Alabamians were not accustomed to doing.

Dr. Rose and I reached an understanding that I would assume the deanship the following summer. So, as had been scheduled, I spent the 1965–66 academic year on a Fulbright Lectureship in

England. This proved to be both an advantage and disadvantage. It was a disadvantage in that it made it slower and more difficult to communicate with Dean Harrison and the faculty at Tuscaloosa; nevertheless we did carry on helpful correspondence. The advantages were that those months gave me an opportunity to reflect on the situation in the law school—what needed to be done there—in a more detached way than I might have done while actively teaching at Virginia. Also, it gave me access to numerous leading English and Scottish law professors and the opportunity, as will be mentioned later, for unusual faculty recruitment. And it broadened and deepened my understanding of the origins of our legal order, inherited from that cradle of the common law.

Against the background of having been a student in the law school at Alabama from 1948 to 1951, I thought that my experiences since then gave me an understanding of the mainstream of American legal education and a sound basis for analyzing the needs of a high quality law school—a year at the Harvard Law School, eight years on the Virginia law faculty, active participation in annual meetings of the Association of American Law Schools (AALS), and a year amidst English legal institutions. Also, I had served on American Bar Association accreditation committees to evaluate the law schools at Duke and Vanderbilt. I realized, however, that every law school is different and that what should be done at Alabama had to be tailored to the situation there and in conjunction with the faculty.

The 1960s were challenging times for Americans and especially in Alabama. For its future, the state badly needed enlightened, well-educated leaders. Throughout history, much of American leadership, for better or worse, had come from the legal profession, and so it had been in Alabama. This was impressively shown by some figures: at that time law school alumni constituted about 75 percent of the practicing Alabama bar, the entire membership of the state Supreme Court, 80 percent of the trial and appellate judges, 15 of the 35 state senators, 40 of the 106 state representatives, six of the state's eight congressmen, both U.S. senators, and the governor. The law school was truly the incubator of Alabama's public leadership. In my mind, strengthening the school and moving it on to more national recognition was important to provide a high quality legal education for the future, which could possibly be the key to giving the state the leadership it should have. I thought of the school as a kind of West Point for the future leaders in Alabama law and government. This gave me a sense of urgency, with no time to waste, when I arrived in Tuscaloosa and became dean on July 1, 1966.

At that time, in the wider world of American legal education the University of Alabama Law School was perceived as being in the company of most other Southern state university law schools, which was to say that it was viewed as more or less respectable though not outstanding. But for nearly a hundred years, as the only accredited law school in the state, the school had been an honored institution in Alabama society, supplying the bulk of the legal profession in Alabama. It had long been accredited by the American Bar Association and a member of the Association of American Law Schools. In the eyes of some observers, however, the school had slipped into what could be described as a state of "insular lethargy." Despite that image, numerous graduates in the late fifties and early sixties—as well as in years gone by—became outstanding lawyers and public servants, proof that real talent will manifest itself. The school's perceived status in the American legal education community pained me, and I was determined to do something about it. At the outset, it was essential that I get an accurate and realistic assessment of the situation.

In my student days (1948–51) the school had seemed a livelier place than it did in the summer of 1966. Back then there had been Dean William M. Hepburn, sophisticated and learned, one of my all-time favorite figures in legal education, who left to become dean of the Emory Law School; Herman Trautman, a dramatic teacher of evidence, who left for the Vanderbilt law faculty; Sam Earle Hobbs, an erudite and polished teacher, who left to join his father in law practice; and a couple of young stimulating teachers, whose names

I have unfortunately forgotten. Also, the post-war surge of returning veterans continued, providing some colorful and interesting
students. But by the summer of 1966 the school had drifted into a
quiet period.

Lack of national visibility was a problem. As far as I could tell,
the law faculty took little or no significant part in the activities of
major national legal organizations such as the AALS, the American Bar Association, or the American Law Institute.[1] A very few
did attend the AALS annual meeting from time-to-time. Lack of
adequate travel funds was partly responsible. Moreover, compared
to law faculties at what were considered "the best" law schools,
published scholarship, with very few exceptions, was slim. [2] That,
along with the lack of activity at the national level, meant that the
faculty was little-known outside of Alabama. Being known on the
national scene was institutionally important in attracting superior
students, recruiting able teachers, and aiding graduates in securing
positions with law firms and government agencies.

On the internal side, what I heard from students and former
students about their classroom experiences gave me concern about
the nature of some of the teaching. Instruction in a good law school
is basically reformist. That is, in addition to imparting to students
the existing legal doctrines and rules, the reason for every rule needs
to be examined and two questions asked: "Does the rule still make
sense?" and "Is there a better way?" Perhaps the most important
question in law school is "Why?" My sense was that there was not
a great deal of this sort of discussion in the Alabama Law School
classrooms. There were exceptions, of course. From random student
and alumni comments that came to my attention, there appeared
to be two or three professors, possibly four (opinions varied), who
were considered effective classroom instructors, some viewed
as very good.[3] Most of the teaching faculty appeared relatively
undistinguished, either in reputation beyond the school or in the
classrooms within it. Yet they were good people, and among them
there were admirable individuals who were sincerely dedicated to

the school and to what they were doing. At the same time, among most, there appeared to be little ambition to alter the situation, to strive to advance the institution. The status quo seemed satisfactory. I was pleased, however, to find a few who appeared ready to join me in moving to a higher plane.

During my deanship I never publicly voiced criticisms of the existing faculty or of what had gone on before my arrival. I did not want to offend those who were already there. Moreover, I wanted to encourage them to look upon this time as the beginning of a new day for the school, an opportunity to advance our place in legal education. Yet it was essential that I have a clear-eyed awareness of reality in order to know what to do. It made no sense to pretend that all was well.

I have described here the image and status of the school as I found it so that readers can understand what I did or attempted to do over the ensuing four years, an account of which follows.

Every aspect of the school deserved attention—its faculty, curriculum, library, student life, and alumni involvement. All aspects had to be dealt with simultaneously, not in sequence. My objective was to move the school to a higher level of quality in every respect—to achieve a degree of national eminence, at least to create the best law school between Charlottesville, Virginia, and Austin, Texas. Why, I asked myself, shouldn't the law school be regarded in the field of legal education as the football team was regarded in the world of college football? The challenge was daunting and uphill, but without that as the goal I would not have accepted the deanship. At stake, in my mind, was a future bench and bar and public leadership that would take Alabama into a new and better day.

Underlying all else was the need to secure substantial funding beyond state appropriations, and that was my immediate priority.

2

THE LAW SCHOOL FOUNDATION
AND LAW ALUMNI

A group of interested alumni had established a Law School Alumni Association in the late 1940s. It mailed out an annual placement booklet and an occasional newsletter and held a luncheon at the annual meeting of the state bar. Those were all useful activities that served to foster institutional attachment. But the association had not undertaken any serious fund-raising.

Before my arrival the most valuable and farsighted step concerning private financial support was the creation in 1961 of the University of Alabama Law School Foundation. It is a nonprofit corporation whose mission is to receive, manage, and expend funds from private sources for the benefit of the law school. A leader in its creation was David J. Vann, who had been a year behind me in law school, also clerked for Justice Black, and was later mayor of Birmingham. He had obtained from me a copy of and largely followed the charter of the University of Virginia Law School Foundation.[4] The University of Alabama Law School Foundation's board of directors included an impressive array of able Alabama lawyers.[5] But like the Alumni Association, it had not been actively engaged in fund-raising.

Because the foundation was a legal entity with tax-exempt status and an organized structure, I saw it as more promising than the alumni association as a vehicle through which we could secure substantial private support. However, the foundation would work in collaboration with the alumni association; the association president

was an ex-officio member of the foundation board. Thus, energiz-
ing the foundation to launch a major campaign was one of my top
priorities. Substantial private money was the key to moving the law
school forward. Happily, the board rose to the challenge without
hesitation. In the early fall of 1966, it resolved to mount an aggressive
capital campaign and adopted an ambitious goal of $1 million. The
campaign and the goal were endorsed by the University of Alabama
Board of Trustees in November 1966.[6]

Although the foundation's board included some of the best lawyers in the state, I thought broadening and diversifying its membership would increase its influence and prestige and enable it to reach
more funding sources. Two ways to accomplish this were to bring
in prominent lawyers who were alumni of other law schools and
to include directors from outside Alabama. I thought these moves
would also make the board seem less provincial.

To that end, over the next couple of years the board elected as
directors: Douglas Arant of Birmingham, Truman Hobbs of Montgomery, and Irving M. Engel of New York, all Yale Law graduates;
Marx Leva of Washington, J. Asa Rountree III of New York, Inzer
B. Wyatt of New York, and Robert E. Steiner III of Montgomery,
all Harvard Law graduates; and Claude E. Hamilton Jr. of New York
and Prime F. Osborn III of Jacksonville, Florida, both Alabama law
alumni. All of the out-of-state directors had Alabama connections
and thus a special interest in helping in this unprecedented campaign
to create a superior law school.[7]

In my first years, Sam W. Pipes III of Mobile was president of the
foundation. He was succeeded by Edward M. Friend Jr. of Birmingham. Members of the board regularly attended its periodic meetings
and tackled the fund-raising challenge with enthusiasm. Foundation
leadership rested in its executive committee.[8] Those busy lawyers
devoted an extraordinary amount of time to law school concerns.
Among them, Howell Heflin—later to become chief justice of the
Alabama Supreme Court and still later a U.S. senator—deserves
special mention. He had been president of the foundation and had

just come off a year as president of the Alabama State Bar. He had boundless energy and a deep interest in the law school. During the years of my deanship he spent more time on law school matters than any other alumnus. I marveled over how he could do it along with his law practice in Tuscumbia.

Primary targets of this fund-raising drive were law school alumni and families of deceased alumni. A difficulty we faced was the lack of a long-established tradition of charitable giving in Alabama and the South generally. The devastation of the Civil War and decades of depressed economic conditions had meant that there was little money for such. The situation was in sharp contrast to that in the Northeast where fortunes had been accumulated and private phi- lanthropy was well-established. But since World War II, the South was becoming relatively affluent. Lawyers' incomes were providing them with discretionary funds that had been rare before the war.

Another difficulty was the widespread view that a state law school should be maintained by the state legislature and that private funding was unnecessary. Overcoming that view and the lack of a philanthropic tradition involved an intensive educational effort. At the numerous bar association meetings and luncheons to which I was invited I took the opportunity to explain why state funds alone were not sufficient. Frank Rose and I stumped the state together with this message, appearing in the six largest cities. Our message had an evangelical fervor. Private funding was necessary to provide a "margin of excellence," as Virginia Dean Hardy Dillard had put it. The public law schools of greatest distinction in the United States—for example, Virginia and the University of Michigan—relied heavily on private support.

Dr. Rose took me with him to New York to discuss the law school with representatives of the Ford and Carnegie foundations. We laid before them our aspirations for Alabama to become a leader in lifting Deep South legal education and research into the first ranks. But the law school never received a grant from either of those sources.

Otherwise, results from the Law School Foundation's invigorated efforts were not long in coming. In the previous year, 1965–66, the foundation received $8,900 in contributions. In 1966–67, contributions increased more than seven-fold to $68,000. At the same time, the University-provided funds also jumped, as Dr. Rose had promised. For 1966–67, the law school budget was set at $407,308, compared to $315,501 the year before. These greatly enhanced financial resources from the combination of state and private money gave the school a boost, suggesting that it was on the way to a new level. There was a sense of real momentum.

A FORTUNATE DEVELOPMENT at this moment was the election of Judge Seybourn H. Lynne as president of the Law School Alumni Association. Chief Judge of the U.S. District Court in Birmingham, Lynne was the most respected legal figure in Alabama. Within the foundation board there arose the idea of asking him, in his capacity as alumni president, to lead a newly organized and energetic annual giving program. We knew that most judges normally would not participate in fund-raising campaigns. But we hoped that with all of the fresh forward movement in the school, he might view this as a special case. I was dispatched to ask him to do this. From my short time in law practice in Birmingham, Judge Lynne and I were acquainted. I had appeared before him in a couple of matters and had met him on a few other occasions. We got along well, and I was one of his many admirers.

We met in his chambers. I updated him on developments in the law school and our aspirations for heightened excellence. I explained our ideas for the annual giving campaign and the reasons for it, saying that we hoped that once it was established it would be a permanent feature of the alumni association. The plan was to appoint a chairman for each class, to solicit his classmates; there would be competition among the classes to see which could produce the highest percentage of contributors. Essentially all we were asking him to do was to sign a letter to all alumni explaining the program and urging them to contribute. At the end of a good discussion, he said, to my great relief and pleasure, "You know my position on fund-raising, but I will make an exception here."[9]

So with that, we launched the annual giving program in 1967–68. At the end of the year, the class of 1931, with W. Inge Hill of Montgomery as its chairman, came in first with 66 percent of its members participating, an extraordinary level of involvement among institutions of higher education. The widespread regard for Judge Lynne was undoubtedly an important factor in the success of that year. But once organized as it was, the program could carry on effectively into future years. Judge Lynne was succeeded as association president by Oakley W. Melton Jr. of Montgomery (my classmate and third-year roommate).

Another idea advanced at that time came from several former law clerks to U.S. Supreme Court Justice Hugo Black who were now practicing law in Alabama. They proposed to establish an endowed fund to commemorate the thirtieth anniversary of his appointment to the Court. Having myself been a law clerk to Justice Black, I immediately supported the idea. He was the law school's most prominent alumnus (Class of 1906) and, of course, was nationally known. The hope was that a fund in his name would attract contributions from his admirers all over the country, reaching resources beyond Alabama. This effort was launched in 1967.

My memory is fuzzy on the details, but somehow arrangements were made for a reception in the White House at which the fund's establishment would be announced. Unfortunately, on the eve of the event President Lyndon B. Johnson had to leave for Germany to attend the funeral of Konrad Adenauer. But the reception went off as scheduled on April 25, 1967, with Lady Bird graciously presiding in the president's place. Vice President Hubert Humphrey gave an eloquent tribute to Justice Black, who was present. I presented him with a certificate from the Law School Foundation announcing the establishment of the fund. Hoping to stimulate interest among the guests, we had placed copies of a printed brochure describing the fund on tables in the State Dining Room, where the reception was held. This event gave the law school some much-needed national visibility.

Since 1954 when Justice Black joined the opinion of the Court in *Brown v. Board of Education*, he had been ostracized in Alabama. But that feeling was melting away. In the summer of 1968 he was invited to speak at the annual meeting of the Alabama State Bar in Tuscaloosa, and he accepted. This was a historic and somewhat emotion-filled moment, as he had not been back in his native state for well over twenty years. The Law School Alumni Association took advantage of the occasion by holding a luncheon in his honor at the University.[10]

THE NEXT SIGNIFICANT development in our seeking enhanced financial resources came in 1968 when George Burns joined the University Development Office. In line with Dr. Rose's commitment to the law school, Burns was assigned to help with our fund-raising work. He came from California where he had been involved in successful fund-raising activities for several colleges. He presented the foundation board with an idea which he said had worked effectively in California. The idea was to establish a selective organization of prominent lawyers and outstanding citizens from other fields, each of whom would pledge to contribute at least $100 annually to the Law School Foundation. This was an especially appealing proposal in that it would draw non-lawyer support, in keeping with our theory that the importance of the law school went beyond the legal profession and was a vitally important institution to the welfare of the state and for the preservation of government under law.

The board agreed with the idea and in the spring of 1969 established the Farrah Law Society. The name honored Albert J. Farrah, dean of the law school from 1913 to 1944, who was much beloved by students who had studied under him. This was at the time, as will be described later, when the Order of the Coif replaced the Farrah Order of Jurisprudence as the school's honor society. So the new society kept the name Farrah alive and satisfied the older alumni.

The foundation board chose Howell Heflin as the society's chairman.

Selective membership was to be by invitation, creating what some might have called an "elite" organization, thus making membership more attractive and creating an incentive to join. Recruitment of members was to be by means of private dinners all over the state, hosted mainly by foundation directors but also by other alumni enlisted for the organizing effort. Twenty-seven dinners were hosted in all parts of the state. I attended all but three. Heflin attended more than twenty.

The project succeeded beyond all expectations. The original goal was 350 members by the fall. That goal was soon passed, and a new goal of 400 was set. That goal too was passed, and membership continued to grow. By the time of the inaugural dinner in Birmingham on October 24, 1969, membership totaled 576. That black-tie dinner was the high-water mark of our fund-raising efforts over the past three years. The principal speaker was Dean Bayless Manning of the Stanford Law School.

Over the next few weeks membership reached 612. Each member was presented with a handsome laminated wooden plaque, numbered, inscribed with his name, and signed by the chairman of the society, president of the foundation, and dean of the law school. With every member pledged to contribute at least $100 annually, this meant a yearly income for the foundation of at least $61,200, in addition to other contributions. To me, this development was a resounding vote of alumni confidence for what had been done in the law school in the past three years and for the direction it was taking. In 1968, after expenses, total foundation assets were $335,429, a figure unimaginable a couple of years earlier.

From a twenty-first century vantage point, the sums mentioned here may seem small. But in the late 1960s they were significant. The law school's annual tuition for in-state students was only $450. Experienced law professors throughout the country were paid less—often much less—than $20,000 annually. Although the foundation's efforts over these four years were a huge boost to the school, it was disappointing that no major gift was received, no blockbuster gift of at least several hundred thousand dollars, no gift at the level the Atlanta lawyers had talked to me about.

GEORGIA WAS ON my mind as we progressed with our fund-raising efforts. I wondered how we compared with that law school. This was a matter of special interest since, as earlier reported, I had been briefed on their grandiose aspirations in January 1964. I found out on November 18, 1967, when I participated in an elaborate dedicatory ceremony to mark the opening of their renovated and enlarged law school building. The principal speaker was Justice Black. The impact of the Atlanta money was obvious. In addition to an excellent building, they had established endowed professorships and lectureships and had expanded the library collection. Of course, they had a three-year head start on us. They also had a governor giving them strong, affirmative support, something we did not have. That scene in Athens strengthened my determination to equal and exceed what I saw. If they had done it, why couldn't we?

As a further step toward unifying the alumni and heightening their sense of institutional attachment, we undertook, with foundation financial support, the first-ever publication of an alumni directory. This turned out to be a more substantial project than had been envisioned. In some instances, records were surprisingly incomplete. Much research was required into University archives and law school files, but eventually every graduate was identified. The effort resulted in the publication in 1970 of the *University of Alabama Law School Directory of Graduates, 1872–1970*. As the title indicates, persons who attended but did not graduate were not included. The directory covered the entire history of the school, from its opening through the class of 1970. It included a list of all faculty members from the beginning, and all graduates, both living and dead, listed alphabetically and by class, with a geographical listing of the living. It is an important reference work on law school history, providing information not readily available elsewhere and certainly not available in any other single publication.[11]

To summarize, nearly everything that had to be done to lift the law school to a higher level depended on securing substantial private funds. Nothing was of higher priority. I estimate that over the four years of my deanship at least half of my time was spent on fund-raising—traveling to attend alumni gatherings and to meet with prospects, writing letters, on the telephone with foundation board members and others. Fund-raising was rarely out of my mind. It was an almost messianic obsession. But I thought it essential to overcome long years of inattention and to catch up with the best of the law school world. Though often stressful and tiring, it was interesting and enjoyable because of the associations it involved with foundation board members and other alumni. They were the strongest source of support. Their enthusiasm for the law school and the time they invested in fund-raising, though they were busy practitioners, was impressive. I was and always have been deeply grateful to them. Without them, much of what was accomplished during those four years would not have been accomplished.

This is a good point to mention the role of my wife, Jan. Throughout the four years of my deanship she was heavily involved in law school activities. The foundation board met regularly in Tuscaloosa, and she nearly always held a reception for the directors at our house. She was particularly good at alumni relationships. We had faculty members to dinner from time-to-time, and Jan assisted in entertaining visiting lecturers and professors. She participated in the Law Wives activities and enjoyed that association. For occasions generally, she served as unofficial law school hostess. She was a great asset to the school and to me; she could hardly have done more.

3

Faculty

The heart of any law school is its faculty. On them depend the nature of the curriculum, the quality of instruction, the general tone of the place, and the school's reputation. In the academic year 1965–66 there were thirteen full-time faculty at the University of Alabama Law School.[12] Most had been on the faculty for over ten years, several for more than twenty. As I saw the situation from my perch in England, the faculty needed to be enlarged in order to expand and enrich the curriculum and to bring in fresh blood to provide a wider range of perspectives on the law.

As mentioned earlier, the law school's budget for 1966–67 was substantially increased. That made possible the addition of several faculty positions. Dean Harrison and the faculty agreed that I should be involved in filling those positions. Because my being in England would make it impossible for the faculty and me to participate jointly in this process, I proposed, and they agreed, that I undertake to recruit some visiting professors in Britain, postponing for another year appointments on a more permanent basis. With that in mind, I attended the annual meeting of the Society of Public Teachers of Law, the British counterpart of the AALS, and consulted with some senior law professors I had come to know. The result was that I obtained two visiting teachers from Britain and one from Australia.[13]

When I returned to the states in June I discovered by happenstance that Wythe W. Holt Jr. had just graduated from the law school at Virginia and was interested in teaching. I had known him as an outstanding student since he first entered law school. The upshot was that I recommended him, and the faculty agreed, for appointment as an assistant professor.[14] He was the first appointee of my deanship to a tenure track position. As it turned out, he was also only one of two persons appointed to the faculty during my deanship whose entire career was spent at Alabama. He became an able, well-recognized legal historian.

Having tapped successfully into the British Commonwealth market, over the next three years we attracted two more visiting professors from England[15] and two from Australia.[16] Thus in my time the law school had seven teachers from elsewhere in the common-law world, widening the legal perspective for Alabama students.

After the 1966–67 academic year, a group of the faculty and I regularly attended the annual AALS meeting, something few of the faculty had been doing in past years. A much increased travel budget made this possible. In December 1968, for example, twelve faculty members were at the AALS meeting in New Orleans. Our main purpose was to recruit young law teachers to fill those new positions on a permanent basis. In a hotel room at those meetings we interviewed several dozen prospects each year. We had their resumes in advance and could do some initial screening. We tried to make the case that ours was a law school on the move and that it presented an attractive place to teach and study. Several of our offers were turned down. In the end, over a three-year period we appointed seven new assistant professors[17] and three associate professors.[18] All had strong academic records from some of the nation's best law schools. Most showed a promising interest in scholarly research.

In addition, I visited several law schools each year, schools that were the main sources of able young law teachers. Competition for top quality was stiff from other law schools. Those recruiting experiences and those at the AALS meetings brought home to me how far the Alabama Law School had to go to be considered by outsiders as in the league with not only the best but also with the very good law schools. It was clear that until we built the school up it was unlikely that we could hope to entice well-established law professors to make a so-called lateral move to join us. Our best hope was to begin at the entry level and work up. We had been fortunate to do as well as we had.

A MAJOR IMPEDIMENT to our recruiting efforts was something we could do nothing about—the reputation of the State of Alabama. In the late 1960s, it was bad. This was not primarily a matter of ideology, of liberal or conservative political views. Across the board, Alabama was looked on as being backward, unenlightened, and intensely racist. When I informed friends and acquaintances around the country that I was taking a position at Alabama, there was often a shaking of heads and rolling of eyes. In the face of such a negative image, all we could do was try to convince others that this heightened the challenge and opportunity to build a well-educated and sophisticated legal profession in the state and that the law school was dedicated to that end.

The combination of our new appointments and the visiting professors meant that the teaching strength of the faculty now varied from nineteen to twenty-three, up from thirteen in 1965–66.[19] We also increased the number of adjunct instructors.[20] The larger faculty had significant benefits for the curriculum, as will be mentioned below, and the new appointees injected an invigorating freshness into the intellectual life of the school.

Still more teaching manpower was necessitated by the important curriculum decision to install a required writing and research program for all first-year students. Imparting those basic skills to law students could not be neglected. The regular faculty members were each carrying a full teaching load; most could not also take on an intensive instructional task of that sort. The solution was to appoint each year four young lawyers from major Birmingham law firms to teach writing and research on a part-time basis. Two regular faculty also participated. Thus we were able to divide the first-year class into six sections. Each instructor was responsible for one section. The Birmingham attorneys came over regularly to meet with the students and supervise their work. Over the period of my deanship, a total of eight young lawyers were thus employed.[21] All were graduates of the top law schools in the country. From all accounts, this writing and research program was successful.

UNIVERSITY OF ALABAMA LAW SCHOOL FACULTY
JULY 1969 ON THE STEPS OF FARRAH HALL

FRONT ROW: Samuel A. Beatty, Harry Cohen, Dean Daniel J. Meador, John C. Payne, and Visiting Professor Neill H. Alford Jr. from the University of Virginia. SECOND ROW: Guy T. Huthnance, M. Leigh Harrison, M. Clinton McGee, Thomas L. Jones, and Igor I. Kavass. THIRD ROW: Wythe W. Holt Jr., C. Dallas Sands, Richard G. Singer, Phillip J. C. Mahan, Julian B. McDonnell Jr., and W. Taylor Reveley III. NOT PICTURED: Gerald R Gibbons, Richard M. Goodman, James B. Kobak Jr., Jay W. Murphy, L. Vastine Stabler Jr., and Visiting Professors John F. Bleechmore and Colin F. H. Tapper.

4

Academic Program

C urriculum and faculty are interrelated. The former is de-
pendent on the latter, and the latter determines the former.
Increasing the number of faculty, as we were doing, permitted a widening of the range and diversity of subjects taught and kept
individual faculty teaching loads at reasonable levels. This growth
also allowed existing faculty to move into new areas of interest.

The relatively small pre-1966 faculty meant that few electives
were offered. Faculty teaching had to be devoted to the traditional,
hard-core, required subjects: Torts, Contracts, Property, Criminal
Law, Constitutional Law, Commercial Transactions, Corporations,
Conflict of Laws, Evidence, and Taxation. The trend in American
legal education at that time was toward allowing students greater
leeway in choosing subjects after the first year. With an enlarged
faculty we moved in that direction. The third year was made almost
entirely elective, the only required offerings being Commercial
Transactions, Legal Profession, and a seminar. The second year
was also opened up to some electives. Professor Samuel A. Beatty
chaired the faculty curriculum committee which kept the course
offerings under continual review.

Civil Procedure presented a difficult curriculum problem because
of Alabama's arcane system of common law and equity pleading;
law and equity remained divided with unreformed intricate pleading rules. For years separate law and equity pleading courses were
understandably considered necessary to prepare students to practice
law in the state. But that then left Alabama students unexposed to

the modern procedural systems used in most of the country, and it reinforced the outdated system, as students knew of no better way and lacked interest in change. Thinking it imperative to do something about this, we made the two pleading courses electives and introduced a new five-hour required course in Civil Procedure in the first year. This gave our students the kind of modern procedure course that was increasingly being adopted by law schools across the country.

I taught a section myself of another new first-year course, Introduction to the Legal Process. It replaced a course called Legislation. It contained elements of that course—examining how courts interpret statutes. It also focused on the almost mystical common-law decisional process whereby the decision in each case builds on cases gone before, requiring the judges to synthesize their holdings to discern a rule that can then be applied to resolve the dispute at hand—maintaining continuity with the past while evolving the law to meet new conditions. As Justice Holmes put it, the law must be stable, yet it cannot stand still. Strong, fundamental, and necessary stuff for first-year law students!

It was my belief, one shared by most law school deans, that it is important for the dean to teach at least one course each year in order to maintain his academic credentials (in contrast to being seen as purely an administrator) and to keep intellectually in touch with students. For me, one of the most fascinating aspects of a career in law teaching is the realization that when I am standing in front of a room full of law students, I know that in that room are future leaders of the bar, state and federal judges, state legislators, members of Congress, and high-ranking executive officials. In short, the future leadership of our society is right there. Of course, we do not know who they are, which individuals will become what. Only in the fullness of time will that be revealed, and when it is, it is enormously satisfying. In no other calling is one privileged to the same extent to address directly day after day such a concentration of those who are destined to be high-level participants in law and government.

And in my life as a law professor, teaching in the first semester of the first year has always been my favorite. There I am writing on a clean slate. Most of those in the first-year classroom know little or nothing about the law, its processes and concepts, so a special challenge rests on the instructor to lay the appropriate foundation and get students started on the right foot. Our new course on Introduction to the Legal Process was ideally suited for this purpose.[22]

EVERY LAW PROFESSOR should be alert to take note of ethical questions whenever they arise in his course, so that students understand from the outset that the practice of law is shot through with ethical conundrums. Moreover, professors need to offer advice about what makes good lawyering. I once heard Lord Kilmuir, Lord Chancellor of England, head of the British prosecution team at Nuremberg, say that he had dealt with lawyers all over the world and that the best of them will always ask two questions: "What are the facts?" and "What does the other side say?" I always thought that worth passing on to students.

Upper-class electives introduced during this time included Admiralty, Comparative Law, English Legal Institutions, Legal History, Legal Reasoning, Law and Higher Education, Law and Poverty, Patent, Trademark & Copyright Law, Private International Law, and Regulation of Competition.

Following up on the first-year writing and research program, we installed a second-year required program in appellate advocacy. In many law schools a large majority of students participated in a voluntary moot court competition. But that had not been true at Alabama. Only ten students had taken part in moot court the year before I came. So we concluded that steps were needed to ensure that all students received this experience. Each second-year student was required to write a brief and present an oral argument. The program was under the direction of Richard G. Singer, a recent faculty appointee.[23] He tackled the assignment with enthusiasm, giving lectures on the techniques involved.

Beyond that required program, we thought it important to have a structured voluntary moot court competition for interested second-semester second-year students and third-year students. Because of its substantive content—training in research and writing and advocacy—such a competition is an important part of the academic program, not merely an "extra-curricular" activity. Giving the competition a prestigious name—that of a distinguished Alabama appellate advocate or judge—would, as it does in many law schools, enhance its status and attractiveness to students. After perusing the field, I concluded that John Archibald Campbell most admirably met the criterion. He was a nineteenth-century Alabama lawyer who was a nationally known appellate advocate and an Associate Justice on the U.S. Supreme Court.[24] So was born the John A. Campbell Moot Court Competition.

The educational experience of such a competition would be enhanced by placing its management entirely in the hands of a student board, membership on which would be considered an honor. The board members would organize and administer the competition, act as judges in the early rounds, and secure the judges for the final round. Designing the cases to be argued gives the board members a significant learning experience. They must identify an emerging legal issue, not yet settled, with opposing arguments fairly balanced, and structure a record that makes possible the presentation of the issue to an appellate court.

Teams of two students would compete in rounds, with elimination down to two teams for the final round. That oral argument would take place during the annual Law Day in the spring, before three judges, mixed state and federal, both alumni and non-alumni.

We installed a large bronze plaque in the courtroom on which the names of the winning team would be placed each year. Robert D. Thorington of Montgomery presented to the law school an oil portrait of Justice Campbell, which was hung in the courtroom.

Also in the courtroom, high on the wall behind the bench, we hung large metallic seals of the State of Alabama and the United

JOHN A. CAMPBELL MOOT COURT COMPETITION
FARRAH HALL COURTROOM—APRIL, 1969

Presentation of portrait of Justice Campbell by Robert D. Thorington, standing at right of portrait. On the bench to judge this final round are Judge Talbot Smith, U.S. District Court (E.D. Mich.); Judge Richard T. Rives, U.S. Court of Appeals for the (old) 5th Circuit; and Justice James N. Bloodworth, Supreme Court of Alabama. The finalist judges in 1967 were: Walter P. Gewin and John C. Godbold, both of the U.S. Court of Appeals for the (old) 5th Circuit, and Aubrey M. Cates of the Alabama Court of Criminal Appeals. In 1968 the judges were: Robert B. Harwood, Supreme Court of Alabama; Seybourn H. Lynne, U.S. District Court (N.D. Ala.); Inzer B. Wyatt, U.S. District Court (S.D.N.Y.). In 1970, two of the 1967 judges sat again: Judges John C. Godbold and Aubrey M. Cates, joined by Judge Frank McFadden, U.S. District Court (N.D. Ala.).

States. Obtaining the latter had not been easy. We were able to get the federal seal only through the intervention of Walter P. Gewin, one of our most active alumni and a judge on the U.S. Court of Appeals for the (old) Fifth Circuit.

This rejuvenated interest in appellate advocacy resulted in the law school's entering a team in the national moot court competition for the first time in several years.

AN ADDITIONAL NEW curriculum requirement was that every third-year student take a seminar. Seminars provided added experience in research and writing, as each student had to submit a substantial paper. Seminars also afforded an opportunity for interaction with a professor in a small group setting, usually a dozen students. This requirement meant that the number of seminars had to be increased.

New seminars, introduced as faculty growth permitted, included Comparative Law, Constitutional Litigation, Correctional Law, Criminal Sentencing, Family Law, Juvenile Courts, Law and Psychiatry, and Legal History.

As in law schools generally, the electives and seminars that were offered depended heavily on faculty interest. They were subjects that a professor wanted to pursue as a matter of scholarly commitment. However, in discussions with faculty members about what they would teach, I did try to steer them toward subjects that I thought were helpful additions to the curriculum. My ambition was to ensure that our curriculum was keeping abreast with developments in the law and that we were exposing our students to the same material offered in the best law schools. In other words, I did not want Alabama students to be left behind in the jurisprudence of the day.

Some of these new offerings reflected the growth in importance of criminal law during the 1960s as a result of U.S. Supreme Court decisions according criminal defendants increased constitutional rights. Going with the spirit of the times, we obtained a grant from the National Defender Project to establish the Alabama Defender Program, under the direction of Professor M. Clinton McGee, assisted by Sam Beatty. This program gave law students actual experience in the defense of criminal cases, mainly during the summer. Although something of an innovation then, clinics of this sort, affording practical training to law students in various fields, soon became commonplace in American law schools.

A MAJOR OBJECTIVE in expanding the academic program was to broaden the perspectives of Alabama law students by exposing them to a wide range of views from elsewhere in the United States and abroad. To that end, in addition to the visiting professors, we invited an array of diverse visiting lecturers each year. This was something new, and it added a stimulating dimension to the life of the school, for both students and faculty. Each lecturer typically stayed three days and gave one lecture, conducted one or more classes in a subject of his choice, and met informally with students and faculty.

Between 1967 and 1970 these lecturers included George Cold-stream, Permanent Secretary to the Lord Chancellor, London; Hardy C. Dillard, University of Virginia; Arthur Goodhart, Master, University College, Oxford;[25] Charles O. Gregory, University of Virginia; Willard Hurst, University of Wisconsin;[26] Paul G. Kauper, University of Michigan; Ormand W. Ketcham, juvenile court judge, Washington, D.C.; Monrad G. Paulsen, Columbia University; William L. Prosser, University of California; Leon Radzinowicz, criminologist and law professor, Cambridge University; and Andrew S. Watson, psychiatrist and law professor, University of Michigan. These were some of the leading figures in the Anglo-American legal world of the day.

Beyond the educational value these lecturers gave our students and faculty, I saw another benefit for the law school. Each could become a means of spreading the word about the University of Alabama Law School. Having been with us and seen our build-up, movement, and aspirations, those influential scholars could enhance our presence and reputation on the national scene. This in turn could help us in future faculty recruitment, attracting able students, and funding from national foundations.

Funding for these lectures came entirely from the Law School Foundation. The lectureship program would not have been possible without that funding source, a dramatic illustration of the difference private support made in the quality of the academic experience. My hope was to underwrite the lectureship program on a permanent basis through an endowment. Giving it the name of a prominent donor might add to its prestige among outsiders and make it easier to attract outstanding lecturers. But we were not successful in achieving that funding goal.

A LAW REVIEW is an integral part of the academic program. Membership on its editorial board provides superb training in research, analysis, and writing. Thus I was especially interested in the status of the *Alabama Law Review*, fueled in part by having been an editor-in-chief in my student days. For many years after its founding, Professor Leonard M. Trawick had been its guiding light. He spent an inordinate amount of time in meeting face-to-face with student editors, going over with them drafts of their case notes and comments, and editing with them. Students who experienced this hands-on treatment remember it as the most educational activity that they had in law school. Trawick has to be considered the founder of the *Law Review* and deserves great credit for that contribution to the school. But in 1966 he had been dead for two years, and there was no member of the faculty inclined to take on that work on a long-term basis.

Moreover, every other law review with which I was acquainted was entirely in the hands of its student managing and editorial board. The time had come, I thought, for our *Review* to move in that direction, out from under faculty supervision.

For that to happen, board members had to be trained in managing, editing, and publishing. In short, we needed someone schooled in law review work to train the board. To fill that role, Wythe Holt was named faculty advisor and began working toward putting the *Review* entirely in student hands. He was succeeded in that transitional process by W. Taylor Reveley III.[27] Both Holt and Reveley had been on the editorial board of the *Virginia Law Review*. The transition to student autonomy was completed during the 1968–69 year.[28] Reveley wrote a detailed memorandum for faculty enlightenment. Topics addressed were: basic objectives of a law review, steps to produce a student-run review, content and frequency of issues, office facilities, finances and the like, and faculty relationship to a student-run review. Along the way, the *Review* began publishing three issues a year instead of two, and printing was moved to a professional law review publisher. The result of these developments was to lift the quality and prestige of the *Review* and to make membership on its board a more sought-after distinction. The year 1968–69 marked the end of the Trawick era, which involved a high degree of faculty supervision, and the start of the new era of a student-managed and -edited journal.

While the *Review* was dedicated to publishing articles of national and international interest, it established an Alabama Section in 1968. There it would publish pieces of special significance to Alabama law.[29] We developed the idea of a student-conducted field research project each summer. Two student board members would investigate the actual functioning of some state legal institution or legal doctrine, and their empirical report would be published in the Alabama Section. This project would be funded by the Law School Foundation, another illustration of the impact of private funding on the educational experience. The first such project dealt with backlogs in Alabama appellate courts.[30] The next project focused on the office of probate judge.[31]

ALTHOUGH THE TERM "globalization" had not yet become fashionable, it was clear in the late sixties that there were increasing international dimensions to the law and that it would be important to the lawyers of the future to be aware of other legal systems. Our appointment of visiting professors and lecturers from other countries was a move to meet that concern. To further the school's international connections, we established a one-year graduate program of study leading to the degree of Master of Comparative Law. It was designed for students from elsewhere in the world who had completed the study of law in a university in their home country and who wanted to experience American law study. The program would benefit our students by allowing them to become acquainted with students from abroad. The program was inaugurated for the

1969–70 year. Its first applicant, and the only one admitted for that year, was Inge Prytz from Denmark. She later emigrated to the United States and eventually became a U.S. District Judge for the Northern District of Alabama.

Promoting study abroad for our own students was one of my interests. As a beginning, I conceived the idea of securing money to send a student to England for the summer. Having spent a year there, I thought that an examination of English legal institutions— the ancestor of our legal order—would be an unusually enlightening experience for an Alabama law student. With that in mind, I approached Earl McGowin of Chapman, an Alabama undergraduate alumnus and Rhodes Scholar, to provide the funding. To his great credit, he readily agreed. A wealthy lumberman, McGowin had served in the Alabama legislature and also held important executive positions in state government. A faculty committee selected one student for this award, from among several applicants.[32] The program turned out to be more elaborate than I had imagined. In addition to meeting with law professors in Oxford and legal practitioners in London, the recipient pursued a course in European art and architecture, with three weeks in England and three weeks on the continent. On his return, he submitted a detailed written report on this extraordinary educational experience. My hope was that this would become a permanent summer program with general Foundation support.

In the summer of 1969, four law students pursued educational programs in Europe through other means, an encouraging international involvement of our students that had not occurred before.

5

Law Library

E arlier I mentioned that on assuming the deanship in 1966, my immediate priority was to activate the Law School Foundation board to aggressively raise funds from private sources. Top priority for whatever money that could be raised was the law library.

In those days, before computers and electronic databases, bound books contained the sources of law and the basis of law study and legal research—reports of court decisions and opinions, statutes, administrative regulations, and treatises and texts. Along with its faculty, its library was the heart of a law school. In 1965 66, the total library collection of those materials at the University of Alabama Law School amounted to 56,000 volumes, small in comparison with many other law schools.

Enlarging the collection was important for two reasons. One concerned the students. With the introduction of the first-year writing and research program, the second-year appellate advocacy program, and the third-year seminar requirement, student use of the library would increase substantially. Ready access to the books, in terms of their number and physical location, was necessary. Perhaps the most heavily used set of books was the National Reporter System. Consisting of several thousand volumes, it contained reports from all state and federal appellate courts and some trial courts. The library held one set and urgently needed to acquire a second. Similarly, multiple copies of the most frequently used hornbooks and other treatises were needed. It is frustrating and wasteful of time to go to the shelf to get a resource and find it not there.

The other reason for enlarging the library concerned the faculty. While the existing collection could be considered minimally adequate for teaching, it was not adequate for in-depth research. Broadening and deepening the collection in at least several fields was necessary to permit the faculty to make the kind of scholarly contributions expected of a good law faculty and to attract new, able recruits. Prospective faculty members of the quality we sought needed to be assured that the library could support their interests.

The Law School Foundation met the challenge with surprising rapidity. In February 1967, the board authorized the expenditure of $40,000 for books. State funds provided the same amount, so we had $80,000 for new acquisitions that year. We then purchased a second set of the National Reporter System. During 1967–68, the Foundation board authorized another $71,000 for books. During 1968–69 the Foundation provided $21,000 for acquisitions. Thus, over a two-year period private support for the library amounted to $132,000. This unprecedented surge in non-state funds, which continued but at a somewhat smaller rate, resulted in growth of the library holdings over this four-year period as follows (as of July 1 each year):

YEAR	VOLUMES
1966	56,302
1967	63,800
1968	78,898
1969	91,000
1970	102,861

Periodical subscriptions increased from 400 to 600.

With the assistance of Congressman Armistead I. Selden, we managed in 1967 to have the library named a U.S. Government Depository. This meant that we could select to receive on a regular basis without charge an enormous array of government publications. At my request, Professor John C. (Jack) Payne,[33] chairman of the faculty library committee, went through lists of hundreds of publications available and chose those he thought most useful to our faculty and students. Payne had long had a keen interest in the library, and I relied on him in that connection. On one occasion he accompanied me to Mobile to call on a major donor to make a special pitch for library support.

SOON AFTER MY arrival the library administration began to give me concern. It seemed to be in disarray. Hundreds of new acquisitions had never been removed from their mailing containers. Many hundreds more had not been catalogued. Moreover, the library staff had apparently not been equipped to make appropriate acquisition decisions. Instead, that task had been performed for many years by Jack Payne, who had a strong interest in the development of the collection.[34] The library owed much to him for being as good as it was.

To gain a third-party perspective on the situation, I invited Frances Farmer to survey the library personnel and administration. She had been president of the Association of American Law Librarians and was then head law librarian at the University of Virginia. Her report, submitted after three days on the premises, confirmed my unease, and I decided that changes were needed if we were to move toward the enlarged and improved research collection that we envisioned.

Igor Kavass turned out to be the man for the job. During 1966–67 he had been a visiting professor from the University of Melbourne in Australia. He had shown a sophisticated knowledge and interest in law libraries and had taken a hand in resolving the cataloging backlog. So in 1968, when it became evident that the library needed new leadership, we brought him back as Director of the Law Library. Getting him back into the country for this purpose was not easy. In the end, I had to go in person to the U.S. Department of Health, Education, and Welfare in Washington to get him cleared.

Kavass was an unusual figure on the Alabama scene. He had been born in Latvia and as a child had migrated with his family at the end of World War II from Latvia to a displaced persons camp in Germany. From there the family moved to Australia. He had a distinctive accent; it was not Australian but not markedly European either. There was about him a kind of Eastern European shrewdness, and he was a keen observer. More than any faculty member, he kept me informed about what others on the faculty were doing and thinking. His major intellectual interest was in foreign and comparative law.[35]

Kavass undertook an energetic and imaginative supervision and development and reorganization of the collection. He was exactly what the library needed. With my approval, he visited numerous University law libraries to gain insights into what the best of them were doing. Working with him was the assistant librarian, Kathleen Price.[36] They made an effective team. They not only made dramatic additions in the number of books but also carried out carefully tailored acquisition policies, filling gaps in existing sets and beginning to build in new areas. They arranged for much-needed additional shelving for the rapidly growing collection, eventually containing three sets of the National Reporter System. They did this by installing free-standing shelves in the main reading room, just off the circulation desk area. This was done in a way that minimized loss of seating in the room. Still more shelving was installed on the unfinished top floor of the 1964 addition to Farrah Hall. They also radically reorganized the physical arrangement of the library to make it more efficient, relocating the circulation desk and periodical collection and creating new reading areas. They introduced the Library of Congress classification system, then sweeping the country. The backlog in processing and cataloging new acquisitions was cleared up and a system put in place to keep that process current. All in all, after two years ours had become a fundamentally different and improved library.

EVEN SO, THE library faced daunting challenges in space and personnel. Annual acquisitions were anticipated to be between 10,000 and 13,000 volumes. At that rate shelf space would be exhausted in a couple of years. Moreover, in number and location, seats for readers were inadequate. All of this gave special urgency to our request for a new building, about which more later.

The staff of eight, not all of whom were professionally trained librarians, was stretched thin. It was difficult for them to man the circulation desk, perform all user services, conduct book selection, and process and catalog new acquisitions. Twenty part-time student assistants helped, but they were no substitute for professional staff. We requested more staff positions, but none were authorized in the University budget.

Student demand on the library had increased to the point that longer hours were necessary. It was rewarding to see this demand, as it indicated greater commitment to the academic enterprise. But we had insufficient personnel for extended hours. We took the unprecedented step of simply leaving the library open twenty-four hours a day, seven days a week, without any overnight or weekend supervision. This was done at first on an experimental basis. Despite the lack of security and staff supervision, it worked well; no problems surfaced. So it was continued, much to the satisfaction of the students.

6

Admissions and Enrollment

When I arrived in July 1966, I discovered that Dean Harrison alone had been reviewing and acting on all applications for admission to the law school. This was a novel arrangement to me, as in every law school with which I was acquainted, admissions were handled by an admissions director or a faculty committee or a combination of the two. With the huge challenges lying ahead, I could not foresee having time for such a task. Moreover, I thought it wise for faculty members to have a role in selecting the students they would be teaching and that the collective judgment of a group on the acceptability of an applicant is better than the judgment of one person.

Accordingly, I appointed a four-member faculty admissions committee, chaired by Professor Harry Cohen (later designated Director of Admissions). They would evaluate and act on every admission application. The committee's decision to grant or deny an application would be final.

Having set up this process, we needed to establish standards for admission. The four committee members and I consulted at length on this. We readily agreed that standards needed to be tightened. This necessity was indicated by the attrition rate of more than 30 percent in recent years. To have nearly a third of the students fail or withdraw was wasteful in terms of time and money for both students and faculty. We thought that an applicant should present evidence of having pursued substantive college courses and having done better academically than barely passing.

Raising standards would inevitably result in more applications being denied than in the past. This was a ticklish matter. As a state institution, the law school had an obligation to provide educational opportunity to a wide range of students. We did not want to risk a political charge of "elitism." Moreover, at a time when we were doing everything possible to cultivate the alumni and overcome the non-tradition of financial support, we did not want to alienate them by denying applications from their sons, daughters, and relatives. We were walking a tightrope. Nevertheless, we were clear that those concerns should not deter us from adopting standards that would reduce attrition and improve the overall quality of the student body. The question was how to articulate heightened standards that would give the committee workable guidance without putting it in a straitjacket.

One important decision had already been made. Through correspondence from England with Dean Harrison and the faculty, I had recommended, and they agreed, that henceforth a bachelor's degree would be required for admission. This change, announced in the spring of 1966, eliminated admission on the basis of three years of college. This step was in line with the practice in many American law schools, a step eventually taken by all.

Our key decision on standards was that an overall average on undergraduate work of at least C+ (1.5 on a 3.0 scale) would be required. C-level work in college would no longer be enough. This average was to be calculated on the basis of courses of "substantial intellectual content," disregarding grades in courses such as physical education and hygiene. The committee was given leeway to admit students with an average less than C+ if there were extenuating circumstances, such as an unusually high LSAT score, suggesting that the applicant was likely to do satisfactory law school work. These new standards were set out in the law school catalog with greater specificity than before. We wanted to convey a sense that standards were being raised and to make it plain that applicants were expected to present a record of relatively solid academic achievement, something more than barely passing, but without drawing a tight line.

A deadline of May 1 was set for applications for admission in the following September. This step hardly sounds radical, but a firm deadline was new. The deadline would allow the committee time to make an unhurried judgment and to enable the formation of a coherent entering class. Again, there was leeway. Late applications could be considered if accompanied by an explanation of circumstances beyond the applicant's control. All in all, we felt satisfied that the adoption of this admission structure and process with strengthened standards would produce good results, allowing collective faculty judgment on the merits of each applicant, reducing attrition, and giving us a class of qualified students.

Realizing the public relations problems that this change in admission standards might pose, I took the opportunity, in addressing the annual meeting of the Law School Alumni Association in July 1967, to explain the reasons for what we were doing and to ask the understanding of the alumni.[37] I pointed out that heightened standards were in the long-range interest not just of the law school but of the legal profession and the public. I was prepared to take the heat. But in the years ahead, the unhappy calls and letters, provoked by rejections of applications, were far fewer than I had expected.

ANOTHER IMPORTANT ADMISSIONS-RELATED decision that had been made in the spring of 1966 concerned the academic calendar. It had been the same since the Second World War. At the close of the war the school went on a year-round calendar. Students were admitted three times a year—in January, June, and September. This was done to accommodate the pent-up demand from returning veterans of the armed services—those who were coming back to complete an interrupted law school career or to begin one. This arrangement was entirely understandable and laudable, and it obtained in almost every American law school. But by the mid-sixties the justification for that academic calendar had long gone.

The year-round calendar had three problems. One was pedagogical. It meant that many students would begin the study of a subject at mid-point. For example, a student entering in January would likely be taking Torts II and Contracts II without having had Torts I or Contracts I. And those students would have had no Procedure. The system made for an incoherent curriculum structure.

The system also adversely affected class coherence and unity, making student life in the school less organized; it retarded long-range class attachments. For example, it was not clear whether a student entering in January was a member of the class that entered the previous September or the one which entered the following June or September.

There was also an adverse effect on faculty life. Under that calendar, most faculty members taught year-round. This left little time for serious scholarship and publication. This lack of time was one reason, though not the only one, why there had been relatively little scholarly production within the Alabama faculty. Serious scholarship usually called for a summer free of teaching duties. The obligation of a law faculty—especially in a public law school—to contribute to the understanding and improvement of the law was unlikely to be met without adequate time for study and reflection. But there was a downside to the elimination of summer teaching: it meant a reduction in faculty income. My plan to meet that consequence of the new calendar was to provide summer faculty research grants with Foundation funds.

For all these reasons, the time had come to end the year-round calendar and admit a new class of students only in September. Fortunately, Dean Harrison and the faculty agreed with me, through correspondence from England, and they had announced this change during the spring of 1966. This put us in line with most other law schools in the country. They, like Alabama, had gone to a year-round calendar right after the war but had now abandoned it. A summer session would remain, offering a limited number of electives for students who had completed the first or second year.

Under the new system, the entire first-year class would assemble as a body on a specified date in September for an opening orientation session, have a welcoming meeting with the dean and faculty, and register for the same courses. This first-year orientation eventually was extended to an entire week, involving lectures on the legal process, a tour of the library, and introduction to student organizations. The class would go through all three years together, taking the same required courses at the same time, although, of course, with variations in their electives in the upper-class years. My expectation was that this arrangement would impart a heightened sense of class coherence and future class attachment as time passed, and thereby, to be mercenary about it, strengthen participation in the alumni annual giving program.

IN ADDITION TO upgrading admissions standards and procedures, it was necessary to tighten academic standards for retention and graduation. The situation in recent years had been a bit loose. The study of law was supposed to be on a full-time basis—no part-time students. Yet it was not uncommon to find students enrolled for less than the required number of semester hours. We made it mandatory for every student to take a full course load every semester. The semester hours required for graduation were raised from eighty-six to ninety. The grading system was refined to make clearer the distinction between marginal students—those in danger of failing—and those that were solidly passing. A student on academic probation had been allowed two semesters to regain good standing. We cut this to one semester. Students had been allowed to drop a course up to the eve of the examination. We prohibited withdrawal after the first week of classes. Students had been allowed to take a grade of Incomplete on the failure to submit required work. We stopped that practice and thereafter, in that circumstance, a failing grade was required. All in all, these changes compelled a greater degree of commitment to the academic enterprise and showed an institutional intolerance for a lesser effort.

After the tidal wave of returning World War II veterans had

receded, law school enrollments nationwide declined substantially. At Alabama as elsewhere, the enrollment slump continued into the early 1960s, when it began to turn around. From an enrollment of 182 in the fall of 1962, it increased each year, reaching a high point of 408 in the fall of 1966. Thereafter enrollment declined as a result of stiffened admissions and retention standards. In the fall of 1967 total enrollment was 342; in the fall of 1968 it was 296; in the fall of 1969 it was 315. The following shows the admissions pattern from 1966 to 1970.

	1966–7	1967–8	1968–9	1969–70
Applications Received	291	254	276	285
Applications Approved	260	214	189	233
Applications Denied	31	40	87	52
First Year Students Enrolled	137	137	123	149
Average LSAT	506	529	529	528
Average GPA	1.5	1.7	1.7	1.7
Voluntary Withdrawals	29	25	14	22
Exclusions (academic deficiency)	28	31	15	17

As this table shows, the average GPA and LSAT scores rose slightly from 1966 to 1967. This resulted from our strengthened admissions standards. Though salutary, the improvement was small. We were proceeding cautiously and not raising standards too high too fast, as previously discussed, because of the politically sensitive nature of access to the state's law school.

The table also reveals that the elevated admissions and retention standards did not serve to reduce attrition until 1968. Then it dropped to a quarter, down from the nearly one-third that it had been for several years. My guess is that the reason attrition did not drop a year earlier is that the admissions committee became a bit more rigorous after a year's experience under the new standards. The result was disappointing; I thought losing a quarter of the class was still too high.

ALTHOUGH SOME THIRTY colleges and universities were represented in the student body during that time, approximately half of the students had done their undergraduate work at the University of Alabama. The other main feeders were Auburn University, Birmingham-Southern College, and Spring Hill College. There was, of course, nothing wrong with Alabama undergraduates, but we thought that the academic experience of all would be enriched by a wider range of backgrounds.

To that end, we began sending faculty members to speak to students and pre-law advisors at other colleges, mostly in the Southeast. Our message was that Alabama was a newly dynamic place at which to study law.

Scholarship funds were essential in this effort. The state provided none. All scholarship money had to come from private sources. Here again the Law School Foundation made the difference. Scholarship funds provided by the Foundation rose from $5,400 in 1965–66 to $17,300 in 1967–68. In 1968–69, the figure was $22,900, with scholarships for 22 students. In 1969–70 the total rose to $32,550, with 39 students receiving scholarships. Most scholarships were in the range of $1,500 annually, based primarily on need. (Annual tuition was under $500.) The one purely merit award was the Holland M. Smith Scholarship. It paid $2,500 annually from a fund established in the will of famed World War II Marine Corps General "Howling Mad" Smith, a law school alumnus.[38]

Establishing endowed funds, the income from which could be used for scholarships, was an attractive naming opportunity for some donors. By 1969 there were ten named funds held by the Foundation.[39] Encouraging the creation of such funds was a continuing part of our fund-raising efforts.

The class entering in the fall of 1969 had two noteworthy features. It included ten women. Since 1963, it happened that only four women had been in each entering class. In earlier years the number had been no higher.

The class also included eight black students. Only one black student had previously enrolled, and he had been excluded for academic deficiency at the end of his first year.

The new black enrollees resulted, at least in part, from my visits to Tuskegee Institute, Miles College, and Stillman College to speak to their students. It was apparent that the economic barrier to those black students' attending law school was almost insurmountable. Scholarships would be essential if we could expect many to enroll. After thinking about how to deal with this problem, I contacted A. G. Gaston of Birmingham, probably Alabama's leading black businessman, and he met with me in my office for a lengthy discussion of the need.[40] Then I flew to New York to see Irving Engel, a lawyer and member of our Foundation board, and explained the situation to him. The upshot was that together Gaston and Engel committed $5,000 annually for scholarships for the next three years. Ed Friend, president of the Law School Foundation, is due much credit for encouraging Gaston to provide this aid. Ed's son, Eddie, then a law student interested in increasing black enrollment, worked with the faculty admissions committee in evaluating black students' applications.

7

STUDENT LIFE AND ACTIVITIES

R ecollections from my student days, reinforced by what I observed within months of my arrival, gave me the impression
that many students were insufficiently dedicated to the study
of law and too little involved in the life of the school. Among the
half of the students who had done their undergraduate work at the
University of Alabama, there was a tendency to remain connected
with that world to the neglect of law school life. This was another
reason for diversifying student backgrounds. Historically—dating
back to the English Inns of Court—law students had been considered part of the legal profession, though not yet members of the
bar. I felt strongly about that concept and believed in that old saw,
often quoted by Dean Farrah: "The law is a jealous mistress . . . he
who would win her must woo her persistently . . . he must live like
a hermit and work like a horse."

The challenge was no less than to change the culture of the institution. Not an easy task. My first step, as previously mentioned,
was to have a well-organized orientation session for the entering
class. Before instruction began, the entire first-year class assembled
in the courtroom—impossible before because of the three-times-
a-year admissions practice. I gave them a welcoming talk, stress-
ing that they were now beginning three years of preparation for a
lifetime career in the law, that the law was a demanding profession,
that law study required more intense effort than many might have
been accustomed to, and law school meant more than just attending classes. Involvement in the life of the school was an important

part of legal education. I introduced the faculty, and that evening we held a reception for the students. My hope was that this would start them off with a sense of class unity and cohesion and a realization that they were now entering a new phase of their lives, stimulated to approach the work ahead with enthusiasm. I tried to stress that the law was more than just a business, that it was a high calling, dedicated to service to others and to society.

AMONG THE STUDENTS I found an incorrect impression that there was a clear distinction between curricular and extra-curricular activities. The life of a law student involved both. So-called extra-curricular activities were important to a well-rounded legal education. It was necessary to get that concept across. But to make the message effective there needed to be a sufficient array of worthwhile student activities to engage the interest of at least most of the students.

A Student Bar Association had long existed. I met often with its officers, representatives of the entire student body, and discussed ideas for additional student involvement. There had also long been an Honor System, but it needed rejuvenating. A student committee was appointed to study its procedures and standards and give it a more central place in student minds. The result was a rewritten Honor Code and the establishment of an Honor Court, consisting of five students elected by their fellow students. Chapters of three national legal fraternities and one sorority appeared to be doing well enough.[41]

Eventually we constituted several student committees to meet with their faculty committee counterparts to make known student interests and to bring students more directly into law school affairs. There were student committees on the library, curriculum, placement, first-year orientation, and new building. Another student organization was the Law Forum, whose mission was to invite occasional speakers. The Law Wives Club was an active group and added much to institutional life.

Student support was marshaled for the publication of a law school newspaper. Most good law schools had student newspapers. Such a publication kept students informed about what was happening in the school, giving them an added sense of professional community. Thus was born the *Alabama Law Reporter*. Unlike the *Alabama Law Review*, membership on the editorial staff was open to all students without regard to academic standing. The plan was to publish five issues annually. The first issue appeared in May 1967. Between then and December 1969, twelve issues were published. The well-written articles covered a range of law school activities. In quality and coverage it compared well with other law school newspapers with which I was familiar. It added a useful dimension to student life.

With student groups and organizations multiplying I found it difficult to keep up with them all. But I thought it important for the law school administration to maintain frequent communication with students. To facilitate contact, I created a Student Advisory Council, consisting of the officers of all student groups. Through meeting with that body I could reach them all. Further, to assist monitoring and keeping in touch with the whole range of student activities, I established the position of director of student activities, and designated Vastine Stabler[42] to serve in that role.

To encourage students to socialize in Farrah Hall or simply to hang out there, an attractive gathering place was necessary. The existing one-room student lounge was not inviting. We renovated the space, creating a two-room lounge. One room was furnished with comfortable seating where students could sit and talk or drink coffee. The adjoining room was designed for light reading, and stocked with several non-Alabama newspapers, as well as the state's major dailies and assorted periodicals. An objective here was to make available to Alabama students information and writing far beyond the local publications to which they might otherwise be confined—another effort to enhance a cosmopolitan atmosphere, reducing provincialism. Of course, we could not force students to read those publications, but we could at least make them easily available in a place where they regularly congregated. We also carpeted the entire ground floor rotunda area outside the student lounge, making it much more attractive.

Everett C. Hughes, a sociologist at Brandeis University, had written a book entitled *White Coats*, an examination of student culture at a medical school. He was recommended to me by David Riesman, a Harvard sociologist, with whom I visited to discuss student academic life. I decided that a Hughes-type study of law student culture would be instructive. So at my invitation he spent three days in Farrah Hall mingling and talking with our students. In our several discussions he gave me his observations about how things were and how they might be changed. My recollection is that he said little beyond what I already perceived, but his observations as a complete outsider were nevertheless interesting and helpful. To my regret, he never gave us a written report.

After a couple of years it was clear that law student culture had indeed improved. There was a vibrancy and lively interest in the school that I had not observed earlier. Serious involvement in these various activities brought students more closely into the institution's life, heightened the sense of professional community, and in general produced an atmosphere more conducive to good legal education.

ON THE LIGHTER side of student life, homecoming in the fall had been for many years the major social occasion. The central features were a dance, the Saturday morning University-wide parade, and afternoon football game. On Saturday morning, law students dressed in cutaway coats, gray striped pants, ascot ties, and bowler hats, assembled in Farrah Hall to begin (or continue) alcoholic imbibing. For the parade, beginning around ten, they climbed on a huge flatbed truck, often with their dates, accompanied by Ramus Rhodes and his organ.

Ramus Rhodes was the school's janitor, general caretaker, and Dean's utility man. He had been with the school since around 1934 and was held in affection by all students and faculty. Dressed in formal attire, with his organ on the back of the flatbed, he had been a prominent feature of Homecoming for years. The favorite song, joined in lustily by the students on the truck, was "That Old Time Religion."[43] Drinking continued, with singing and shouting getting ever more raucous, as the truck crept slowly in the parade along University Avenue, past hundreds of onlookers, including the president, members of the board of trustees, and alumni from all over the state. The image of the law school that the spectacle presented did it no credit. In fact, it was an embarrassment to the University.

This situation brought me into an early, but mild, tiff with the University administration. Soon after I arrived in the fall of 1966, Dr. Rose called and asked me to join him and David Mathews, his assistant (and future successor), for lunch. It quickly became apparent that the purpose of the gathering was to ask—not quite order—me to pull the law students out of the parade. Dr. Rose said that for several years he had been getting complaints from influential alumni about the students' unseemly, even disgraceful, conduct. Mathews said little, but nodded affirmatively. This was sensitive ground, and I felt on the spot. It was hard for me to imagine that one of my first acts as the new dean would be to order an end to this long-standing and cherished tradition. Although I agreed that much of the student conduct was undesirable, abolishing the truck ride would surely have gotten me off on the wrong foot. It did add to school esprit, something I was working hard to build. After we discussed it at some length, I said I would talk with the student leaders and make known to them the concerns. But I did not promise to do more. Thereafter I did meet with the student officers and reported on my meeting, letting them know the harm to the University the president perceived in the law students' Homecoming performance. But Homecoming continued as usual. I never heard about the matter again. Looking back, I have wondered whether my response to their request, or failure to respond, had any bearing on what was to unfold three years later.

8

ADMINISTRATION

Administratively, in addition to dealing with student affairs as just discussed, and establishing an admissions committee, as previously described, I perceived a need to coordinate and bring together physically a student records office, admission applications, and placement service. Two rooms directly across the rotunda from the dean's office were the obvious place in which to make these functions readily accessible to students.

One of these, a large room, had been for many years occupied by Professor Jay Murphy. It was a choice location, with a large window affording a view across an expanse of lawn toward the President's Mansion. It was the only faculty office on the main floor; all other faculty were on the floor above with the library. No other area in the building was as suitable for the administrative space that we needed.

Dislodging Murphy would not be a happy task for me, entrenched as he was. With reluctance, I called on him and explained as best I could that the management of these school functions needed a suitable location where they could be coordinated efficiently and made accessible to students. To my great relief and to his credit, he did not protest, although he understandably was not pleased.

After renovations, this was the room in which all student business was handled. All student records were kept there with office personnel. We built a counter just inside the door, separating the files and work area from students and others visiting the office.

We made a connecting room the office of Guy T. Huthnance, the assistant dean and director of placement. He was there to supervise the office and receive students with problems.

Each year the school had been publishing a booklet containing photographs and biographical information about each graduate. This booklet was widely distributed, inviting inquiries from law firms and others who might be interested in employing a graduate. Beyond that, however, there had been little in the way of a systematic placement program. In that time law firms had begun to visit law schools to interview students, but few had come to Farrah Hall. Under Huthnance's direction we tried to stimulate such visits. We mailed out four thousand brochures to law firms and government agencies throughout Alabama and elsewhere in the Southeast, inviting their interest in our students. We wrote letters to selective law firms and agencies all over the state specifically inviting them to send representatives for student interviews. During 1968–69, twenty-one interviewing teams came to Farrah Hall, whereas a few years earlier there had been none. This was also a time before summer employment of first- and second-year students became widespread, so we sent letters urging firms to consider such, especially promoting the idea among the alumni. For the benefit of the students, we published a placement booklet giving advice about seeking opportunities with law firms, government departments, and judicial clerkships. In general, the placement office became a more organized, active, and effective service for both alumni and students.

EARLY IN MY tenure numerous other administrative matters required my attention. For example, I discovered that there was no faculty mail room or any other centrally located place where faculty could receive communications. Incoming mail and memoranda from the dean to the faculty had to be hand delivered by Ramus Rhodes to each faculty member. This was inefficient and time consuming. So I created a small faculty mail room in which each faculty member had a large pigeonhole. Also, using these boxes the faculty could easily send notes to each other. Students could use them to send messages to the professors.

After a couple of years I was beginning to be stretched thin administratively. I was spending about half my time on fund-raising, which often took me away from Tuscaloosa. With our effort to build up the school—the push for excellence—being dean was not a routine administrative job. There was a constant striving to move ahead in faculty recruitment, library development, curriculum enhancement, and the matters already mentioned. In addition, I was continuing the tradition of law school deans everywhere of teaching at least one course each year. The upshot was that I felt the need for more help.

To that end, I appointed Camille Wright Cook as administrative assistant to the dean.[44] One of her immediate assignments was to organize and run an office to handle admissions and scholarship applications. Harry Cohen, now designated Director of Admissions, and his colleagues, serving as the admissions committee, acted on all applications. But they were not equipped to handle the large volume of paperwork. All of that was placed under Camille Cook's charge in an admissions office we created on the main floor in what had been the women's rest room.[45] For years law school applications had been initially processed through a University Admissions Office and then sent on to the law school. That bifurcated arrangement made no sense. With our own Admissions Office in place, it was ended.

We had arrived at a much improved administrative structure with Camille Cook's installation, together with Cohen as Admissions Director, Huthnance as Placement Director, and Stabler as Student Activities Director. Still, administrative responsibilities and pressures continued to grow. To assist me further I appointed Julian B. McDonnell Jr.[46] as an assistant dean. He helped me in a variety of ways, but his main responsibility was to deal with the multitude of individual student problems.

In addition to the library rearrangement already described, and the creation of the admissions and student records offices and renovation of the student lounge, we made several other changes in Farrah Hall. The two-room dean's suite was reversed; the inner room which had been the secretary's office was made the dean's office, and the outer room, which had been the dean's office, became the secretary's room. Carpeted and painted, this became a more appropriate and attractive place in which to receive law school visitors and to meet with small groups of students and faculty. In the empty top floor of a Farrah Hall addition, we constructed new space for the *Alabama Law Review*, a seminar room, and two rooms for the Alabama Law Institute, to be described below.

A YEAR AFTER my arrival, an unfortunate distraction arose in the form of a move to establish another state law school. It was hard to imagine anything the state needed less; there was simply no case for two state-supported law schools. Yet I had to invest substantial time in preparing a brief in support of the opposition and in appearing at hearings in Montgomery. Alex Pow, the University Vice-president for Academic Affairs, worked with me and was strongly supportive. At a time when we were struggling to increase our state funding, we had to take this threat seriously. It would have been disastrous for the state's limited resources to be divided between two duplicating schools. The move finally died, but it had drained off my time from more pressing matters. The episode was disquieting in that it showed that some influential persons in Alabama had no understanding of what a first-class law school required.

THE DIPLOMA THE law school issued to its graduates had long struck me as inadequate. It was unusually plain and did not convey the importance of what it represented. So I, in consultation with several faculty members, undertook to redesign it. We came up with more attractive lettering and a gold University seal instead of one simply printed in black ink—a more impressive "sheepskin" to frame and hang on the wall! The administration approved, so it was adopted.[47]

One of my tedious yet pleasant duties as dean was to sign diplomas on the eve of graduation. The diplomas came over in a batch from a central university office. Each had to be signed by the president of the university and the dean of the law school. President

Frank A. Rose's signature was affixed mechanically, but I signed each personally, with a real pen and black ink. With more than a hundred diplomas, this was no quick or easy job, if error were to be avoided. I sat at a large table in my office signing slowly and with care to avoid messing up. My secretary, Doreen Brogden, spread them out for the signatures to dry. By the time I finished, every flat surface in the office was covered with drying diplomas. Though tedious, this was a satisfying exercise, bringing home to me that we were sending out into the world another group of potential leaders in law and government.

Signing the diplomas for the class of 1969 gave me particular pleasure, as that was the first class to have gone through all three years of law school under my deanship. Most of the changes during my deanship took place during that time. The members of that class were generally supportive of what was being done. They were especially helpful in enabling the school to obtain a Coif charter. For these reasons they hold a special place in my memory and affection.

The 1969 graduation exercises were memorable because my brother, Clifton, who had recently been appointed dean of the Medical School, stood with me on the platform and presented diplomas to the medical graduates. Thereafter the Medical School held its own graduation exercises in Birmingham. Eventually the three University of Alabama campuses—Tuscaloosa, Birmingham, and Huntsville—became separate, autonomous institutions.

When I assumed the deanship there was underway a nationwide movement to change the name of the law degree from Bachelor of Laws (LL.B.) to Juris Doctor (J.D.).[48] The argument was that students entering law school already had a bachelor's degree, so it made no sense to award them another. Law school was graduate work, and the title of the degree should reflect that. I had not been excited over the movement so this change was not high on my agenda. But pressure was mounting, nationally and locally. Deciding to go along, I recommended the change, and the administration agreed.

Because the change was retroactive, we faced the task of issuing replacement diplomas to hundreds of alumni—to any who applied. We developed an application form and required payment of $25. The business was to be handled through the Foundation, which would make a small profit. Each replacement diploma had to be signed by the president of the university and the dean of the law school. So I, as a 1951 graduate, had the unusual experience of signing my own diploma.

IN 1937, THE law school had established the Farrah Order of Jurisprudence, its academic honor society. The national law school honor society was the Order of the Coif, the equivalent of Phi Beta Kappa in the undergraduate world. Student membership in both organizations was confined to the top 10 percent of each graduating class. It was my understanding—but I never verified this—that the reason the school established the Farrah Order was that it had been rejected for membership in Coif. In any case, I deemed it essential that the law school obtain a Coif charter. A law school's membership in the Order of the Coif was a badge of academic quality; it was a kind of "Good Housekeeping Seal of Approval" in American legal education. Only fifty law schools out of the nearly one hundred and fifty in the United States at that time had charters.

Graduating students who had been taken into Coif would benefit because such was a nationally recognized honor, whereas the Farrah Order was unknown beyond Alabama. Faculty would benefit from being at a school with the qualitative status accorded by Coif membership. That status would also help in faculty recruitment. The school's not being in Coif had a negative implication from which it was imperative to escape.

Anxious as I was to secure a Coif charter, I thought it prudent not to move too fast. An application to the national Order at the beginning of my deanship would, in my judgment, have carried too great a risk of an embarrassing denial. Work needed to be done to bring the school along with development in faculty, curriculum, library, and student life. By the fall of 1968, I thought we had progressed to the point that we could risk an application, and the faculty agreed.

Thus we undertook to prepare a petition for a charter, in accordance with Coif rules. This turned out to be a far more elaborate task than had been anticipated. The result was a 121-page document presenting a comprehensive picture of every aspect of the law school.[49] Submitted in December 1968, it began with the following:

> The University of Alabama Law School has entered a new era of vitality and development, with qualitative movement upward in all respects. The objective, being pursued vigorously in every area of the School's program, is to create and maintain a truly superior quality of legal education. Stress is being laid on broadening and strengthening the traditional areas of instruction and scholarship while at the same time expanding the curriculum into new areas of concern with new patterns of instruction.... It is doubtful that the data alone [in this petition] convey the full spirit and import of the accelerated activities in connection with faculty recruitment, library development, curriculum growth, and admissions upgrading, and of the general reinvigoration within the law school.

In April 1969, the Order sent a team of two inspectors to spend three days at Farrah Hall. The team consisted of Professor Frank Strong of the University of North Carolina, former AALS president and dean of the Ohio State Law School, and Professor Thomas S. Currier of the University of Virginia. Realizing the critical nature of their visit, I had alerted all faculty and students to put their best foot forward and cooperate in every way with the inspectors, and all rose to the occasion admirably. The inspectors did a thorough job, talking and mingling with many students and most faculty members, reviewing admissions data, canvassing the library, sitting in on classes, and selectively reviewing examinations and seminar papers.

Approval of our petition was no sure thing in my mind. My apprehension rose when Professor Strong reported to me that one of the examinations he had reviewed seemed to be quite deficient and that some seminar papers were of poor quality even though they had received high grades. I suggested that he talk with the professors involved and that he also interview the entire *Law Review* editorial board. Those were the students likely to be accorded Coif membership if a charter were granted. This he did and was favorably impressed.

To my immense relief, shortly after their visit, Professors Strong and Currier submitted a report to the executive committee of the Order of the Coif recommending a charter.[50] Approval of that recommendation required an affirmative vote of at least eighty percent of the fifty member schools. We could take nothing for granted. It was a banner day when in October 1969 we received official word that we were in—a historical milestone in the life of the law school![51]

Based on the inspectors' discussions with me and on what they said in their report, my sense is that two factors played critical roles in their favorable recommendation. One was the impressions they gained from their interviews with *Law Review* members and from the general enthusiasm and interest of the student body. The other was their perception of the commitment and competence of the faculty that had been appointed since 1966. In short, the students and young faculty carried the day for us.

IN 1967, THE Alabama legislature enacted a bill to establish the Alabama Law Institute, modeled on the American Law Institute and the Louisiana Law Institute.[52] This was a forward-looking measure, designed to provide an agency for continual law reform work. It would be headed by a director, with a governing council. An important question remaining to be decided was its location. Efforts were mounted by our alumni to have the Institute placed at the law school. To our delight, the Council decided to do so at its first meeting in September 1968.

The Institute's location at the law school served significant mutual interests. For the Institute, it provided office space, the resources of the state's major law library, and access to student research assistants and faculty reporters. For the law school, it was a great boon. In addition to the prestige of being home to the Institute, the school would gain additional funds for library acquisitions ($50,000 initially), jobs for part-time student research assistants, and stipends to the faculty for serving as reporters on the various projects. The arrangement made it possible for an able person to serve half-time as Institute Director and half-time as a faculty member. Vastine Stabler, already an associate professor, agreed to serve temporarily as director, drafting by-laws and generally getting the Institute organized. We made space available in Farrah Hall for the director and a secretary.

9

Farrah Hall and a New Building

arrah Hall, the first University building constructed exclusively for the law school, had been the school's home since 1927. It was a solid, three-story structure, looking more or less as a law school should look. When it was built it was one of the most impressive university law school buildings in the South. It stood at the corner of University Avenue and Hackberry Lane, its columned front looking diagonally across the Quadrangle toward Denny Chimes and the Amelia Gayle Gorgas Library. Through its corridors and classrooms for forty years had passed a large part of the Alabama bar, a host of future state legislators and Congressmen, judges (state and federal, trial and appellate), and governors. It had served well the school and the bench and bar. Among alumni there was considerable sentimental attachment to it, which I shared.

Additions to the building along the University Avenue side in 1949 and 1964 provided much-needed new space. The internal renovations improved the situation for the library, administrative services, and student life. But by the late sixties it had become clear that the building would not be adequate for the law school of the future, in light of all that was contemplated.

At my request, a local architect spent several hours going over Farrah Hall with me. He said that when it was built it had an architectural symmetry. But the additions had destroyed the symmetry. He saw no good way that it could be renovated or expanded to accommodate the changes and growth that lay ahead. His opinion reinforced my view that we needed to work toward a new building for the superior school we envisioned, and there seemed to be general faculty agreement.

The first step was to get the university administration to commit itself to a new law school building and give us a green light to commence planning. At this point we were not seeking specific funding or a site or any other details. After considerable talking and pushing we finally obtained such a general endorsement and permission to seek an architect.

My next struggle was to gain permission to engage an out-of-state architect. There was an unwritten rule that for state-funded projects an in-state architect was required. So it was no little accomplishment when we were cleared to go out of state.

My objective, as with everything else connected with the school, was excellence—to construct a truly first-class building, one that would be distinguished as one of the outstanding American law school structures. To that end, I deemed it essential to engage an architect of international renown. That alone would attract attention to the building and give it added cachet. I began the search by talking with several law deans whose schools had recently built new structures. From them I also got advice about plans and design. Beyond that, I undertook a survey of eminent architects throughout the United States. Eventually I identified three with whom I wished to visit in person: Paul Rudolph, Hugh Stubbins, and Edward Durell Stone. All agreed to see me.

Paul Rudolph was an Auburn architecture graduate and former dean of the Yale Architecture School, then practicing in New York City. He was noted for his unique, contemporary style. Hugh Stubbins of Cambridge, Massachusetts, had done numerous academic buildings, including the Loeb Drama Theatre and Countway Medical Library at Harvard. He had won the international design competition for Congress Hall in West Berlin. Edward Durell Stone of New York City had designed the Kennedy Center, then under construction in Washington, and the acclaimed American Embassy in New Delhi, and many other commercial and academic buildings. I spent a day meeting personally with each, looking at models and pictures of his work, and talking with his staff. I stressed that we were not interested in just another academic structure but a building of exceptional architectural distinction. Each seemed interested in the project.

After returning home and thinking it over, I chose Stone. My judgment was that he was the most likely to give us the building we wanted and one that would fit in comfortably with existing university architecture, not an unimportant consideration.

In the meantime, a faculty committee, collaborating with the student new building committee, was hard at work preparing a document that would comprehensively set out our ideas for content and design.[53] It dealt in concepts, not with floor plans. At that time there was emerging the concept of a "law center" in contrast to a "law school." That is the concept the committee pursued. The major element would, of course, be the law school, and in it the library would be the centerpiece. Much attention was devoted to describing what the library should contain and its relationship to faculty offices. Administrative offices, classrooms, and student activity space were all addressed. As a Center, the building would also include the Alabama Law Institute, the State Bar Continuing Legal Education Program, the Alabama Defender Program, and other future clinics and programs. Recommendations were also made for living and dining facilities for law students. The document was appropriately ambitious. Completed in March 1969, it began:

> A basic assumption which must underlie all planning is that we
> are seeking at this institution to create a genuinely distinguished
> law school of national stature which will far exceed in quality the
> typical university law school. This means that the physical facilities
> housing such an institution must be of commensurate stature, as
> judged in both academic and architectural circles.[54]

We provided copies to university administration officials and to Stone. In April he and an associate came to Tuscaloosa. He met with faculty and university administrators. We had a lengthy conversation in my office. I explained my views that a law school should look like a law school; its architecture and interior design and decor should be such that one entering the building would know immediately that he was in a place of the law and not, for example, in an arts or sciences classroom building or a home of engineering or business administration. Symbolism was important, especially in the library, courtroom, and major lobby and corridors. Somehow the eight hundred-year old Anglo-American legal tradition should be physically reflected in the surroundings.[55] Stone seemed receptive to my comments. Thereafter he wrote expressing serious interest, making it clear that he would take on the project, if it were offered. I considered this an enormous tribute to our aspirations, as he had a multitude of opportunities from throughout the world. Eventually the university administration agreed to his employment, but not without considerable persuasion. This was a huge step forward in the law school's quest for national visibility!

But there was not agreement with details. The administration balked at the idea of living and dining facilities for students. In response, I contacted the deans of half a dozen major law schools which had such facilities and received strong endorsements of the concept. They all said this enhanced the legal education experience. I had initially suggested $4 million as the right amount of money to be allocated for the building, but Dr. Rose thought that excessive. But I was not ready to give up on the point. Later I proposed that the project be divided into two phases. Phase I would be the law school and related offices and programs, at a cost of $4 million, and that Phase II be the living and dining facilities, at a cost of $1.5 million. Phase II could be delayed until some future time. I urged that 1972 be the date for either commencing or completing construction of Phase I. I never received any response to these matters.

SINCE 1968 LAW school relationships with the central administration had been getting more difficult. When I arrived and up until

1968, the Vice-president for Academic Affairs had been Alex Pow. He was the person with whom I worked regularly on law school matters, especially the budget, and we hit it off in good style. We saw eye to eye on the school's problems and needs. He was fully supportive of Dr. Roses's commitment to the school. He was the no-nonsense type, getting right to the point. It was a pleasure to work with him. Unfortunately, in 1968 he resigned to become president of Appalachian State University.

That was a turning point in my dealings with the administration. Pow's successor was Raymond McLain, an older man, new to the University. Although polite and easy-going, he had no special interest in the law school and seemed to be unaware of our development and objectives. After his arrival, the law school's annual budget received progressively smaller increases. For example, in 1966–67 faculty positions had been increased to seventeen, and in 1967–68 to twenty, but then there were no further increases, although we had requested twenty-five positions as our ultimate objective. Dr. Rose continued to announce his commitment to the school, but he did nothing aggressively to help our cause. As I saw it, contrary to my hopes, he was not doing for the law school what he had done for the medical school.

To attempt to reinvigorate the administration, I conceived the idea of bringing a nationally recognized figure in American legal education as an independent third party, to survey our entire program, its progress, direction and objectives, and make a report to the president. For this purpose, I invited John Ritchie, then dean of the Northwestern University Law School. He had previously been dean of two other law schools: Washington University and the University of Wisconsin. He had also been president of the Association of American Law Schools. In June 1969, he spent two days in Tuscaloosa examining all aspects of our situation, much as the Coif inspectors had done. He also talked with administration officials. In his written report he gave our program a ringing endorsement. In referring to our faculty committee report on the proposed new building, he said:

> If appropriately implemented, it will lift the law school of the
> University of Alabama to national eminence. It will enable the
> University to retain and to recruit outstanding law professors. It
> will attract to the law school more top quality students and more
> states will be represented in the student body. It will provide a
> legal research center that will make a truly significant contribu-
> tion to the state, the region, and the nation. It will provide a use-
> ful clinical experience for the law student by affording him the
> opportunity under appropriate supervision of serving the legal
> needs of indigents. It will provide a well-rounded program of
> instruction attuned to the demands of contemporary law prac-
> tice and permitting the student who desires to do so to study in
> depth a legal area appealing to him. In summary, it will be the
> leading law center of the South and one of the great law centers
> in this country. [56]

One would have thought that any university administration
would have been delighted to receive such a report and would have
applauded the efforts to develop such a law school, one that would
bring distinction not only to itself but to the entire university and
the state. But there was no such reaction.

In his report, Dean Ritchie noted that he had been made aware
of a suggestion that consideration be given to relocating the law
school to the University of Alabama campus in Birmingham. He
took no position on that idea but recommended that the location
question be studied and resolved before planning proceeded for
the proposed law center. The suggestion had come from some of
the young faculty members. They thought that the resources and
leadership on the Birmingham campus that had built up the Medical School would make that location more promising for the law
school's future. I joined Dean Ritchie's recommendation for a study
in my dean's annual report submitted shortly thereafter. Contrary

to rumors, I never recommended that the school be moved to Birmingham, only that the question be studied. My view was that any
serious suggestion concerning the law school's future should be
given consideration and not rejected out of hand. But the recommendation for a study was promptly rejected by the administration,
and that ended the matter.

During 1969, in addition to the Ritchie report, much else was
going extraordinarily well for the law school, the culmination of
three years' work: chartering by the Order of the Coif—an endorsement of quality from the legal academic world—the huge success
of the Farrah Law Society—a resounding endorsement from the
alumni—and obtaining Edward Durell Stone as architect. Those
events, together with the Ritchie Report, would, I hoped, reenergize
the university's commitment to a superior quality law school. But
that was not to be.

10

DENOUEMENT

T he resignation of Frank Rose as president of the University of Alabama changed everything. The man who had brought me to the deanship with the understanding that we would develop a truly outstanding law school—the man who "would do what he had done for the Medical School"—was now to be gone. Although, as shown earlier, his enthusiasm had been waning, we nevertheless had a connection and relationship that was unlikely to be duplicated. With his successor for the moment unknown, the law school faced an uncertain future.

But we did not have long to wait. In the late spring of 1969, the University Board of Trustees appointed David Mathews as president. He had been on hand as an assistant to Dr. Rose since I arrived, but I was not well acquainted with him. The appointment came as a surprise to many, as Dr. Mathews was young, relatively short on experience, and little known in the world of higher education beyond the local scene. I was a bit uneasy, as he had never appeared to be a cheerleader for the law school, but I hoped that we could get off on a good footing. Sometimes little things help, so Jan gave a tea for Mrs. Mathews.

In the course of that summer Dr. Mathews and I had three lengthy conversations about the future of the law school. My hope was to get him to understand our entire program, what we had done over the past three years, and our grand objectives. The result of these conversations was disappointing, to say the least—disillusioning would be more accurate.

While I do not, of course, know exactly what was in Mathews's mind, I do know what he said and the impressions I received. As I understood him, his message was this: the law school's drive toward national eminence was to be modified. We should reorient ourselves to becoming a good state law school for Alabama. Our objective of attracting more out-of-state students—we had suggested twenty percent—should be abandoned. The school should "come to terms with its past." By this I took him to mean that the pre-1966 faculty should be given greater voice. What I did not know then was that some of those faculty members had been communicating directly with Mathews, voicing their discontent over what was going on in the law school.

As I also learned later, the suggestion of a move to Birmingham had more adverse reaction among those faculty and with Mathews than I could have anticipated. For those faculty long entrenched in Tuscaloosa, the thought of such a move was out of the question. And the idea apparently was seen by Mathews as a threat to his leadership and to the integrity of the Tuscaloosa campus. The recommendation for a study of the location question had injected a discordant note into an already tense atmosphere. It is doubtful that things would have developed differently if the question had never come up, but in retrospect it probably would have been better if it had not.

Mathews's stance puzzled me then and still puzzles me. It was incomprehensible to me that a university president would back off from the achievements and momentum of the law school in this banner year. Mathews never explained the reasons for his position.

In all of this, I saw an undercutting of the hopes and dreams of the many alumni who had worked so diligently to secure financial support, the recruitment of faculty on certain representations and expectations, and all that we had been representing to the students and outside world for the past three years. The assumptions on which I had accepted the deanship were no longer valid. In short, the whole ball game had changed.

THE TURN OF events put me in a painful quandary. The question I had to face was whether I could continue when the reasons why I had taken the position no longer held. Could I comfortably and effectively preside over a law school with lowered ambitions? Routine administration of the status quo was not something I was cut out for. I could foresee constant frustration with the Mathews administration. Would it be fair to the school for me to serve as its dean when my heart was not in the changed policy?

While I was going through this mental turmoil, a development changed the picture overnight. In August, while attending the annual meeting of the American Bar Association in Dallas, I had dinner with Dean Monrad Paulsen and Professor Hardy Dillard of the University of Virginia Law School. Dillard had recently been appointed judge on the International Court of Justice at The Hague and was leaving the faculty. Out of the blue, Paulsen asked whether I would be interested in coming back to Virginia to fill Dillard's position. Dillard seconded the suggestion. I was stunned. This was an extraordinary opportunity, as the position was the James Monroe Professorship, one of the three original chairs at the law school. I was so taken aback that all I could say was that I would love to think about it.

Now I had an intensified dilemma. I had never wanted to be a career dean. When I accepted the Alabama position, I told Jan and a few friends that I could imagine holding it for no more than seven years, but I thought I should give it at least four. I was now beginning my fourth year. If I were ever to make the move back to being a law professor, which I eventually wanted to do, there would be no better opportunity. On the other hand, I felt a strong sense of responsibility to Alabama—to the students, the alumni, the faculty I had recruited, and to the future of the state. I had never been so torn over any decision.

As the fall came on, my decision grew easier when it became even more evident that Mathews and I did not have the same view of the law school and that I would not have his support for what I thought the school should do. My decision was also made easier by two circumstances within the school.

One was the increasing realization that most of the pre-1966 faculty, as I mentioned earlier, for reasons I never understood, lacked enthusiasm for the entire development we were undertaking. This was especially curious because all we were doing was to their benefit—securing greatly increased private support, enlarging the library, adding scholarships to attract top students, enhancing the school's status with the Coif charter, and planning a grand new building. Why any faculty would not embrace this program mystified me. Nevertheless there was that element, and the prospect of going forward with them was not attractive. Unfortunately, there had developed a divide between faculty appointed since 1966 and those appointed before, not a healthy academic environment.

I had always been careful to avoid criticism of the situation in the law school before my arrival, as I did not want to offend the existing faculty. But by advocating change in so many areas I had unavoidably implied that all had not been well. Change is unsettling, and the human tendency to resist it is understandable. But there are only two other choices, neither attractive: do nothing, or creep along incrementally for years. This was a delicate matter and I never resolved it comfortably. In any case, some of the older faculty may have taken offence at much of what was happening, construing it as criticism of themselves.

Also I think the older faculty felt threatened by what they perceived as pressure to publish scholarly research. Such activity had not been part of the faculty culture there. With few exceptions, they saw the job as teaching and little else. But the younger faculty were interested in research and writing, considering it part of the job. Wythe Holt set an early example. Whatever the reasons, it had become clear that most of the senior faculty felt uncomfortable in the changing academic atmosphere and did not share my goals and ambitions for the school but were likely to be in accord with those of President Mathews.

The other circumstance that made my remaining less attractive was the likelihood that several, and possibly all, of the post-1966 faculty appointees would resign because of the changed university policy. That would have left the non-supportive faculty with ever more influence, causing me ever more frustration. That dysfunctional situation would not have been good for the school.

THE RESULT OF this anguished deliberation was that as we came into October I concluded that I should resign. But then I faced the question of timing. The inaugural dinner of the Farrah Law Society was coming up in Birmingham on October 24. In my mind that was to be the joyous culmination of three years of effort with the alumni and a spectacular affirmation of what the law school had accomplished. I feared that announcing my resignation on the eve of that event would cast a shadow over what should be a celebratory evening. On the other hand, to go through the dinner and then announce a resignation soon after would seem deceptive.

As the date approached I talked over the phone several times with members of the Foundation executive committee, explaining that I thought the wisest course was for me to resign. They urged me to withhold final decision. We all met in the late afternoon of October 24 in a room in the Parliament House in Birmingham, site of the reception and dinner scheduled for that evening. We discussed the whole situation again. This was a painful conversation. Here were the men who had worked most closely with me for over three years, not wanting me to leave. They asked me to make one last try with Mathews by calling him then and there and getting a final judgment as to his views on my remaining. It was their suggestion that I tell him of my tentative decision to resign and see whether he in any way asked me not to. Fortunately, I reached him on the phone immediately. We had a brief conversation, and he said nothing to indicate that he wanted me to remain. This was not surprising, as I had thought that was his position all along. When I hung up and reported to the group, they reluctantly agreed that I should announce my resignation that night at the dinner. It would be better to get it out now, as painful as that would be, rather than a day or two hence.

I have never had a more heart-wrenching experience. More than three hundred guests had gathered for this gala black-tie launching of the Farrah Law Society. After dinner, and after Dean Bayless Manning spoke, I rose and gave the expected remarks, congratulating and thanking everybody for the extraordinary effort that had brought us to this point. Then, somehow I was able to say that I was resigning the deanship and tried to explain that my long-range interest had been in teaching and that I had been presented with an exceptional opportunity and that I thought that I had accomplished here much of what I had set out to accomplish.[57] Anything I could have said would have been inadequate. There was no good way to say it. The audience was stunned. No one had any inkling of my decision except the executive committee members with whom I had met that afternoon.

The next day I formally tendered my resignation as dean of the law school, effective June 30, 1970.

As I HAD feared there was in some alumni quarters a sense of having been let down, of having had the rug pulled out from under the hundreds of alumni who had just culminated the highly successful organization of the Farrah Law Society. But from many I received letters and phone calls expressing regret but also appreciation for what the school had done. Especially gratifying was the student response in the form of a resolution, signed by 208 of the 342 enrolled, stating regret over my departure and giving a long list of constructive changes and accomplishments.[58]

To no one except members of the Foundation executive committee did I ever explain the major reason for my resignation, namely, the change in the university policy concerning the law school wrought by Mathews. It was tempting to let the world know the detrimental effect on the institution that would flow from this change. But I thought it would not be in the best interest of the school to bring this out in the open. To do so might generate further controversy and dampen alumni enthusiasm, which I thought essential to be maintained for the school's future.

Then came the spring of 1970 with the usual flurry of end-of-year activities, notably the annual Law Day and the graduation exercises. That graduation was especially memorable, as this was the first graduating class to have experienced the full three years of all the changes in the school that had been made. This gave me a great sense of satisfaction. At the same time, the occasion was touched with sadness. This was the last time I would be signing all those diplomas and presenting them to Alabama Law School graduates. With the handing out of the last diploma, my job would be done.

11

Summing Up

Looking backwards from that academic year of 1969–70 to July 1966, I tabulated the important steps and developments that had occurred within the law school during that time, as follows:

- evolution of the Law School Foundation into an energetic fund-raising entity, supplying the school with substantial private financial support;
- establishment of the Farrah Law Society with its long-range funding commitments, activating hundreds of alumni;
- doubling of the library collection to more than 102,000 volumes;
- reorganizing and upgrading of the law library administration;
- designation as a U.S. Government Depository;
- establishment of a Student Records Office, Admissions Office, and Placement Office;
- establishment of a first-year writing and research program;
- establishment of a second-year appellate advocacy program;
- institution of a third-year seminar requirement;
- inauguration of the John A. Campbell Moot Court Competition run by a student board;
- increasing the number and variety of elective courses and seminars;
- inauguration of a graduate degree program, Master of Comparative Law;
- inauguration of a program of distinguished legal scholars as visiting lecturers;

- initiation of appointments of visiting professors from abroad;
- strengthening and reorganizing the *Alabama Law Review* into an autonomous, student-edited journal;
- establishment of a student newspaper, the *Alabama Law Reporter*;
- upgrading of admissions standards and procedures;
- tightening of academic standards for retention and graduation;
- enrollment of eight black students (only one having previously enrolled);
- heightening student commitment to and involvement in law school life;
- redesigning the law school diploma;
- changing the name of law degree from LL.B. to J.D.;
- publishing first *Directory of Graduates, 1872–1970*;
- providing a home for the Alabama Law Institute;
- obtaining university approval for a new law school building;
- securing approval of Edward Durell Stone as architect;
- securing a charter from the Order of the Coif.

This picture of the law school in June 1970 was strikingly different from the law school of July 1966. Credit for this change is due to hundreds of alumni—and especially to the Law School Foundation executive committee—for unprecedented financial and moral support, without which much of the above would not have happened. Large credit is also owed to the enthusiasm and aspirations of the younger faculty members. Student leaders contributed to a remarkable degree. President Frank Rose must be recognized as opening the way to the entire development. From the vantage point of the twenty-first century, Alabama law professors and students may think the above list unexceptional—features of the school now taken for granted. However, in the context of that time these were huge accomplishments, novel in the law school of the mid-sixties, and brought about only through great and persistent effort.

My hope was that these steps were irreversible. But I was uneasy over the fate of many. My uneasiness was heightened by the resignations of six of the young faculty members,[59] leaving the faculty predominantly as it had been in 1965–66. The 102,000 volumes in the library would obviously remain. However, much else could be neglected, watered down, or abandoned. There was the real possibility that the "great experiment," as some called it, would be dismantled. In any case, it seemed unlikely in the near future that the school would become "the best law school between Charlottesville and Austin." I was satisfied, however, that I had given it all I could, had done the best I could, virtually around the clock for four years, and that under the circumstances it was doubtful I could have accomplished more. I did regret that I would not have the opportunity to see our grandiose plans materialize.

As I departed Tuscaloosa, exactly four years after my arrival, my dominant emotion was sadness—sadness for the bench and bar and people of Alabama, sadness for the current and future law students. There had existed a unique chance that this institution could break out of obscurity—out of the Deep South's willingness to accept second place in the nation—and build a truly first-class training ground for the future leadership of Alabama and the country. But my sadness was tinged with hope—hope that in the fullness of time leaders of vision would emerge and carry forward the dream, bringing to fruition what had been contemplated in the headiness of those transitional years.

THOSE WERE MY thoughts on departing Tuscaloosa more than forty years ago. Now, these decades later, I can see that I was unduly pessimistic.[60] Over time, my hopes had largely prevailed. Alumni interest has not flagged, and evolving law school leadership and faculty composition appear eventually to have brought many of our dreams to fruition.

From a great distance of time and space, I perceive that private financial support has continued and grown substantially; endowed professorships and visiting professorships have been established, as well as annual lectureships.[61] Student scholarship aid has grown enormously; the faculty has been enlarged and diversified and the curriculum greatly expanded. The *Alabama Law Review* is thriving as a student-edited journal, and additional publications have been inaugurated. The John A. Campbell Moot Court Competition, run by a student board, continues, along with other moot court activities. The library thrives. The projected new building, designed by Stone, was constructed, and it was occupied by the law school in 1978. The library space was later expanded, and a new wing added.[62] The school's ranking within American legal education has markedly improved.[63] Though I am not an up-close observer, at the close of the first decade of the twenty-first century it all looks good to me, and I am immensely pleased that our long-ago efforts were not in vain.

In my address to the Alumni Association in 1967, I quoted from Dean Farrah's remarks in accepting the keys to the newly constructed Farrah Hall, exactly forty years before I was then speaking. He promised, among other things, that the building should "perform the great service to the state for which it was designed and thus become a 'veritable temple of learning,' a shrine for real seekers after truth, a Mecca for those who would learn the law."[64]

I concluded by saying that it was our honor in the law school to renew those promises, so that if our present momentum continued, "forty years from now" it could be said that those promises have been kept. Those forty years have now passed. The promises do indeed appear to have been kept. The University of Alabama Law School has gone a long way toward flowering into the institution that was envisioned in those years from 1966 to 1970.

NOTES

1   Two professors were engaged in legal projects with an international dimension: C. Dallas Sands in Liberia and India, and Jay W. Murphy in Korea.

2   The main exception was Prof. John C. Payne, the most scholarly of the pre-1966 faculty. He was seriously interested in legal research and had published several substantial law review articles.

3   There was a consensus across the years that Dean Lee Harrison, Hepburn's successor, was excellent in the classroom. In his courses in Contracts and Conflict of Laws he was a master of the so-called Socratic Method.

4   The Foundation's incorporators were George Clopper Almon, Clifford Fulford, and M. Leigh Harrison.

5   The initial president was Justice Thomas S. Lawson of the Alabama Supreme Court (for whom I had served as law clerk). The first board of directors, in addition to the three incorporators, consisted of Robert B. Albritton, John A. Caddell, Edward M. Friend Jr., Walter P. Gewin, Howell T. Heflin, Thomas B. Hill Jr., W. Dewitt Reams, and David J. Vann.

6   *Law School Foundation Report*, 1967, page before page 1.

7   A list of all directors who served between 1966 and 1970 is contained in Appendix B.

8   In addition to Pipes and Friend, the executive committee included John A. Caddell, Walter P. Gewin, Howell T. Hefflin, George A. LeMaistre, Robert McD. Smith, and myself, ex officio.

9   At my invitation, for the benefit of the Civil Procedure class, Judge Lynne conducted pre-trial conferences in the Farrah Hall courtroom in two cases pending before him in the U.S. District Court (N.D. Ala.). In the years since, it has not been unusual for courts to hold sessions in law schools, but at that time it was rare and novel.

10 At the luncheon, President Rose presented Justice Black with a Phi Beta Kappa key, to replace the one he lost years earlier.

11 The University Office of Development had assigned Col. W. Vann

Brown to run the Law School Foundation office in Farrah Hall, and he supervised preparation of the *Directory*. Marshall Timberlake, a law student in the class of 1970, carried out the research on the graduates. Professor Wythe W. Holt Jr. assembled the historical data on the faculty. Law alumni directories have been issued periodically in later years, but they do not include the historical information published within the 1970 directory.

12 They were: Samuel A. Beatty, Harry Cohen, Harry H. Haden, M. Leigh Harrison, Guy T. Huthnance, Thomas L. Jones, Joseph H. Lawson, Philip Mahan, M. Clinton McGee, E. Dwight Morgan, Jay W. Murphy, John C. Payne, and C. Dallas Sands. Morgan resigned at the end of the academic year 1965–66 to join the law faculty at the University of Oklahoma and thus was not on the faculty when I arrived. Three adjunct instructors had long been on the faculty: Perry Hubbard, George A. LeMaistre, and Judge J. Russel McElroy. J. Jefferson Bennett was carried on the faculty roster, but he was serving as Administrative Vice President of the University. Six of these professors had been on the faculty in my student days, but I had taken courses under only three: Harrison, Murphy, and Payne.

13 John Neil Young (University of Aberdeen), F. E. Mostyn (University of London), and Igor I. Kavass (University of Melbourne). In addition to being a practicing solicitor and law lecturer in London, Mostyn was also a novelist and short story writer, using the pseudonym Bill Mortlock. At my request, he published a short story in the *Alabama Law Review*: Mortlock, "Every Poison Its Own Antidote," 21 *Ala. L. Rev.* 513 (1969). The idea for fiction in a law review came from a short story by Louis Auchincloss to commemorate the fiftieth anniversary of the *Virginia Law Review*: Auchincloss, "The Senior Partner's Ghosts," 50 *Va. L. Rev.* 195 (1965). That was the first original work of fiction in an American university law review; Mostyn's story was the second. The third was another short story: Auchincloss, "Abel Donner," 75 *Va. L. Rev.* 1(1989), marking the seventy-fifth anniversary of that *Review*.

14 Holt was initially appointed as visiting assistant professor but six months later was given a tenure-track appointment at that rank. The faculty also agreed to the appointment of William C. Gifford Jr., a recent Harvard law graduate, to be a visiting assistant professor.

15 David A. Thomas (London School of Economics) and Colin F. H. Tapper (Oxford).

16 Manfred P. Ellinghaus and John Bleechmore, both from the University of Melbourne.

17 James B. Kobak Jr., S. Leroy Lucas, Julian B. McDonnell Jr., Harve H.

Mossawir Jr., Stephen M. Raphael, W. Taylor Reveley III, and Richard G. Singer.

18 Richard M. Goodman, L. Vastine Stabler Jr., and Gerald R. Gibbons.

19 A list of persons teaching full time in the Law School between 1966 and 1970 is contained in Appendix A.

20 Longtime adjuncts—Perry Hubbard, George A. Lemaistre, and Judge J. Russell McElroy—continued. The new adjuncts were Edward M. Selfe and J. Michael Rediker (Birmingham attorneys), Iradell Jenkins (Professor of Philosophy), E. Douglass Lanford (Director of the State Bar CLE Program), and Richard A. Thigpen (Assistant to the University President).

21 John P. Adams, Wyatt R. Haskell, James Lewis, Thad G. Long, Drayton Nabers Jr., James L. North, Henry E. Simpson, and L. Vastine Stabler Jr. That five of these were university of Virginia Law graduates was no accident. Having known first-hand the legal writing and research program through which they had gone, I had confidence that they would understand and implement the program we wanted.

22 The casebook used in this course was Paul J. Mishkin & Clarence Morris, *On Law In Courts—An Introduction to Judicial Development of Case Law and Statute Law* (The Foundation Press, 1965).

23 Singer was a University of Chicago law graduate and former law clerk to Judge Harrison Winter of the U.S. Court of Appeals for the Fourth Circuit. He later served on the Rutgers University law faculty for many years.

24 After being admitted to the Alabama bar, Campbell practiced in Montgomery and then in Mobile. He was appointed to the Supreme Court by President Franklin Pierce in 1853, having been recommended by all of the sitting Justices. Henry J. Abraham, *Justices and Presidents* 30, 111–12 (2nd ed. 1985). Having resigned his seat at the outbreak of war in 1861, he later regained national distinction as an appellate advocate, eventually confining himself to practice in the U.S. Supreme Court. He argued two of the most famous Reconstruction era cases: *The Slaughter House Cases*, 83 U.S. 36 (1873) and *U.S. v. Cruikshank*, 92 U.S. 542 (1876). In the former he argued, albeit unsuccessfully, for a broad interpretation of the new Fourteenth Amendment restricting state action. In the latter, his client's position required an argument to the opposite effect, which he presented, demonstrating the versatility of a skilled advocate. Robert Saunders, Jr., *John Archibald Campbell—Southern Moderate, 1811–1889* (1997).

25 Goodhart, an American, spent his career as a law professor at Cambridge and Oxford. His mother was a sister of Sen. Herbert Lehman of New York. She had been born in Montgomery where in pre-Civil

War days her family was a partner in the Lehman-Durr Drug Company. Goodhart was delighted when I took him to Montgomery and showed him the Lehman-Durr site, the state capitol, and the Alabama State Bar headquarters. A small group of lawyers and judges gave a luncheon in his honor at the Montgomery Country Club.

26 Hurst had a major research interest in the development of law in relation to sectors of economic life. After his visit, following up on that interest, I encouraged research of that sort by faculty and the *Law Review* into the history of Alabama law in relation to fields such as agriculture, timber, mining, waterways, etc. Alabama is rich in possibilities for Hurst-type research. But no one in my time took up the suggestion.

27 Reveley was a University of Virginia law graduate who left academia to enter law practice (eventually becoming managing partner of Hunton & Williams) but later returned to academia as dean of the Law School and later president at the College of William and Mary.

28 The first issue under the new student-run regime was Volume 21, Number 1. The managing board for that volume consisted of the following: Editor-in-Chief, J. Knox Argo; Managing Editor, Fournier J. Gale III; Alabama Editor, Robert L. Potts; Articles Editor, Frank P. Samford III; Comment and Casenote Editors, James A. Harris Jr. and John C. H. Miller Jr.; Research Editor, Howard C. Oliver; Business Manager, Robert H. Smith. That managing board and those that followed remained in office throughout publication of the entire volume, ending the past practice of having the *Review* officers change with every issue.

29 The new Alabama Section was explained in "Editorial Comment," 21 *Ala. L. Rev.* 148 (1968).

30 "Alabama Appellate Court Congestion: Observations and Suggestions from an Empirical Study," 21 *Ala. L. Rev.* 150 (1968).

31 "Office of the Probate Judge in Alabama: His Duties, Qualifications, and Problems," 22 *Ala. L. Rev.* 157 (1969).

32 The recipient was Fournier J. (Boots) Gale III. The runner-up was James C. Davis.

33 Referred to by students as "Black Jack."

34 See Paul M. Pruitt Jr. & Penny Calhoun Gibson, "John Payne's Dream: A Brief History of The University of Alabama School of Law Library, 1887–1980, With Emphasis Upon Collection Building," 15 *J. of Leg. Prof.* 5, 12–17 (1990).

35 Kavass later went on to become head librarian in the law schools at Northwestern, Duke, and Vanderbilt.

36 Price later became the law librarian at the Library of Congress and

head librarian in the law schools at Duke and NYU.

37 This address is contained in Appendix C.

38 At a ceremony to mark the establishment of the Fund, Alabama Marine Corps reservists presented a bronze bust of the general to the Law School. Conrad "Bully" Fowler, Shelby County probate judge, Reserve colonel, and Law School alumnus, presided, in full Marine Corps uniform. I remember the event mainly because my well-laid plan was thwarted. I had arranged for the university band to set up on the parking lot just outside the courtroom a half hour before the ceremony and play a series of Sousa marches, culminating with the "Marine Corps Hymn." But two hours earlier, heavy rain commenced, and the band canceled its appearance—a disappointing loss of a colorful and dramatic feature!

39 The Named Funds were: Hugo L. Black, Marc Ray Clement, Francis H. Hare, Julius W. Hicks, DeVane King Jones, Leon McCord, Gessner T. McCorvey, William S. Prichard, John D. Rather Jr., and Holland M. Smith. In addition, several scholarships were available from other sources.

40 Gaston explained the key to his financial success: "I saw a need, and I filled it." He learned this in his childhood living in a rural neighborhood. There was no swing. He found an old automobile tire and a rope. He tied the tire to a tree limb and charged other children a penny to swing.

41 DeGraffenreid Inn of Phi Delta Phi, John Tyler Morgan Chapter of Phi Alpha Delta, Chi Chapter of Sigma Delta Kappa, and Alpha Ro Chapter of Kappa Beta Pi.

42 Stabler was a University of Michigan law graduate who first served as a part-time instructor in the first-year writing and research program while in a Birmingham law firm. He was appointed an associate professor in 1967. He later returned to law practice in Birmingham.

43 "Gimmee that old time religion . . . it was good for old Dean Farrah, it's good enough for me," and so on.

44 She was a native of Tuscaloosa, a 1947 graduate of the Law School, and had been teaching in Auburn. At about this same time I employed Doreen Brogden as the dean's secretary. She, Camille Cook, Wythe Holt, and Gerald R. Gibbons (appointed in my last year) were the only persons who joined the faculty and staff during my deanship who remained long-term after my departure. They served the school for many years until their retirements.

45 A new women's rest room was created on the ground floor. The number of women enrolled in the Law School then was such that almost all of them could gather in the rest room at one time.

46 McDonnell was a University of Virginia law graduate who had recently returned from service in Vietnam as an Army captain. He eventually found his academic niche at the University of Georgia Law School.

47 I sent a copy of the redesigned diploma to the deans of the Medical and Dental Schools, with the suggestion that they adopt it as well, so that our three professional schools would have uniformly designed diplomas. My recollection is that the Dental School adopted it, but I do not recall what the Medical School did.

48 The leader of the national movement was John Hervey, advisor to the ABA Section of Legal Education and Admissions to the Bar. The J.D. was ultimately adopted by all American law schools.

49 *Petition of the Faculty of the University of Alabama School of Law for a Charter in the Order of the Coif,* December 1968.

50 *Report to the Executive Committee of the Order of the Coif on the Petition of the Law Faculty of the University of Alabama School of Law.*

51 The first students inducted into the Order of the Coif after the charter was granted were members of the Class of 1970: Douglas T. Arendall, David H. Bibb, Joseph T. Carpenter, William D. Hudson, Henry R. Thomas, and Abbott B. Walton Jr. Students in the top ten percent in the classes of 1969 and 1968 were inducted retroactively, as authorized by Coif policy.

52 1967 *Ala. Laws* 629.

53 The faculty committee consisted of Cohen, Holt, Kavass, McDonnell, Meador, Murphy, Reveley, Sands, Singer, and Stabler. Sands served as reporter.

54 *Program and Design Criteria for a Law Center at the University of Alabama—A Prospectus for Progress Toward Distinguished Leadership in Legal Education and Research,* March 1969. Two interesting suggestions, among many, were that there be a Hugo Black room, replicating either his home study or his Supreme Court room, and that there be one classroom furnished with the Farrah Hall classroom seating. That seating consisted of heavy, solid oak benches, said to be modeled on the seating in the British House of Commons. Each bench accommodated two students. With their straight backs and wooden bottoms they were uncomfortable, but they were a significant part of the Farrah Hall tradition thought worthy of preserving.

55 One of my major disappointments, resulting from my departure as dean, was not having the opportunity to follow through with the design of the building, with the hope of having it reflect these views. The extent to which my views are embodied in the building that eventually materialized, I cannot say, as by the time it was con-

structed I had lost my eyesight.

56 *Report on the proposed Law Center at the University of Alabama,* July 1969, submitted by Dean John Ritchie. On reading the quoted passage, I thought, "There, Georgia, what do you make of that?"

57 The text of my remarks is in Appendix D.

58 *Alabama Law Reporter,* Vol. III, no. I, p. 2 (Dec. 1969).

59 They were: Igor I. Kavass, James B. Kobak Jr., Julian B. McDonnell Jr., W. Taylor Reveley III, Richard G. Singer, and L. Vastine Stabler Jr. In addition, John F. Bleechmore and Colin F. H. Tapper, visiting professors, would not be returning. Samuel A. Beatty resigned to become dean of the Mercer University Law School.

60 Apparently we had progressed more than I realized at the time. In Robert B. Stevens, *Law School—Legal Education in America from the 1850's to the 1980's* 213 (1983), Alabama is listed as one of five schools that in the 1960s "came into national prominence."

61 In 1994, I was honored by the Law School's establishment of the Meador Lecture. At the School's invitation I delivered the inaugural lecture, published as "Transformation of the American Judiciary," 46 *Ala. L. Rev.* 763 (1995). Originally designed to present one lecture annually by an outstanding legal scholar, the Meador Lecture later evolved into the presentation of several lectures delivered annually, focused around a central theme. At the end of the year these lectures are reprinted in a single publication. See, e.g., *Meador Lecture Series 2005-2006: Fiduciaries* (three lectures with introduction); *Meador Lecture Series 2007-2008: Empire* (in two volumes, four lectures with introduction).

62 At a groundbreaking ceremony for the new wing on March 18, 2005, I was honored to deliver the principal address at the school's invitation.

63 The law school rankings by *U.S. News & World Report* have long been controversial, their validity and accuracy questioned. But for what it is worth, I note that in 1999 Alabama for the first time made it into the top 50, coming in at number 50. In 2011, Alabama was ranked number 35, tied with Georgia, Ohio State, and Wisconsin. Among public law schools in the Southeast only Virginia and William & Mary were ranked higher.

64 See the concluding passage in Appendix C.

65 This is a private, nonprofit, tax-exempt corporation whose mission is to secure private financial support for the state historical park at Old Cahawba, site of Alabama's first state capital. Cahaba Foundation, Inc., 719 Tremont Street, Selma, Alabama 36701; 334-874-8000; cahabafoundation@bellsouth.net; www.cahabafoundation.org.

Appendix A

Full-time Faculty, 1966–1970

[Years are shown for those not serving the entire time]

Samuel A. Beatty

Harry Cohen

Talbert B. Fowler (1954–67)

William C. Gifford Jr. (1966–67)

Harry H. Haden (1946–67)

Wythe W. Holt Jr.

Thomas L. Jones

James B. Koback Jr. (1969–70)

S. Leroy Lucas (1967–1968)

Julian B. McDonnell Jr.(1968–70)

Daniel J. Meador

John C. Payne

W. Taylor Reveley III (1968–70)

Richard G. Singer (1968–70)

Colin F. H. Tapper (1969–70)

J. Neil Young (1966–67)

John F. Bleechmore (1969–70)

Manfred P. Ellinghaus (1967–68)

Gerald R. Gibbons (1969–)

Richard M. Goodman (1969–)

M. Lee Harrison

Guy T. Huthnance

Igor I. Kavass (1966–67, 68–70)

Joseph H. Lawson (1965–68)

Phillip J. C. Mahan

M. Clinton McGee

Jay W. Murphy

Stephen M. Raphael (1967–68)

C. Dallas Sands

L. Vastine Stabler Jr. (1967–70)

David A. Thomas (1967–69)

Appendix B

University of Alabama Law School Foundation Officers and Directors 1966–1970

[Not all directors served the entire four years.]

President
Sam W. Pipes III (1966–68)
Edward M. Friend Jr. (1968–)

Vice President
Thomas B. Hill Jr. (1966–67)
Edward M. Friend Jr. (1967–68)
Henri M. Aldridge (1968–69)

Secretary
David J. Vann (1966–70)

Treasurer
J. Rufus Beal (1966–70)

Directors

Robert B. Albritton	Henri M. Aldridge
Douglas Arant	J. Rufus Beal
Oliver W. Brantley	Albert P. Brewer
Hubert Burns	John A. Caddell

Irving M. Engel
Edwin M. Friend Jr.
Thomas G. Greaves Jr.
M. Leigh Harrison
Howell T. Heflin
Truman Hobbs
Thomas S. Lawson
George A. LeMaistre
Hugh D. Merrill
Sam W. Pipes III
Charles A. Poellnitz
William S. Prichard Jr.
L. Drew Redden
J. Asa Rountree III
Robert McD. Smith
Inzer B. Wyatt

Peyton N. Finch
Walter P. Gewin
Claude E. Hamilton Jr.
Edwin I. Hatch
Thomas B. Hill Jr.
Mortimer H. Jordan
Alto V. Lee III
Marx Leva
Prime F. Osborn III
T. Virgil Pittman
Walter J. Price
W. DeWitt Reams
Patrick W. Richardson
Thomas D. Samford III
Robert E. Steiner III

Ex Officio

James E. Clark, Alabama State Bar
Richard B. Emerson, Alabama Law Alumni Association
Francis H. Hare, Alabama Law Alumni Association
Seybourn H. Lynne, Alabama Law Alumni Association
Daniel J. Meador, Dean of the Law School
Oakley W. Melton Jr., Alabama Law Alumni Association
Sam W. Pipes III, Alabama State Bar
Robert E. Steiner III, Alabama State Bar

APPENDIX C

ADDRESS BY DEAN DANIEL J. MEADOR AT THE
ANNUAL LUNCHEON OF THE ALABAMA LAW SCHOOL
ALUMNI ASSOCIATION, MONTGOMERY, ALABAMA,
JULY 21, 1967

[Preliminary remarks are omitted]

Today I propose to talk chiefly about academic matters.

This will be a kind of report to the stockholders, or perhaps more accurately, to a partnership meeting, in which I shall attempt to recap some of the highlights of current academic developments in our Law School and to share with you some of our concerns. In a dynamic enterprise of this sort, in a time of transition, it is obviously impossible to do more than give a glimpse of the more significant features.

We can begin with the students. The most obvious fact about our students today is their number. Like law schools nationally, we have gone through three periods since the war. First was the post-war tidal wave which lasted into the early fifties. Then enrollments sagged in the middle and late fifties, at times below the level of the 1930s. The third period, which we are in now, began in the early sixties. In 1962 our total law school enrollment was 180. This past fall it was 400. This is more than a doubling in four years. Increases are predicted to continue, though we believe that the rate of increase will diminish.

We have some excellent and superior students who would do well in any law school in the United States. Unfortunately their numbers are all too small. One of our priorities is to attract a larger proportion of exceptionally gifted young persons. The presence of a significant number of such persons in the school is as important to its overall quality as any other single factor. And of course the quality of the bar is significantly affected by the quality of students coming to the Law School. The main way to attack this problem is through making the total program more attractive to this type of student. This we are attempting to do as fast as possible through curriculum and faculty expansion. Scholarship money is also essential.

Diversification of background among law students is highly desirable for purposes of their own education. The first-year students who began law school last September had attended thirty-four different colleges and universities. We rejoice in having students come to us from this many institutions. Almost every college in Alabama is represented as well as a number of the major universities of America, such as Columbia, Yale, Harvard, Vanderbilt, Duke, Virginia, North Carolina, and William and Mary. However, fifty percent of all these entering students had done their undergraduate work at the University of Alabama. This is an undesirably high percentage to have from any one institution. We need to broaden our base still more. This fall we plan to move in that direction by sending members of the faculty and some of our students to visit selected colleges, to make known to undergraduates the dynamic quality of our growing Law School. Student recruitment has become well established with many law schools, and we must join in. This should result not only in our drawing from a wider variety of colleges but also in our attracting a larger number of superior applicants, both of which will further improve the quality of the educational experience afforded.

Two matters giving us particular concern are our minimum admissions requirements and our academic standards, that is, the standards for remaining in school and graduating. We need your understanding and your moral support as we make changes in these areas which we believe to be in the public interest. The basic point to bear in mind is this. The Law School is a part of a university, a part of higher education, at the post-graduate, professional level. Our job is to prepare men and women intellectually to enter an ancient and learned calling. We have an unusual responsibility to the public. Within the law faculty we are going on the assumption that the legal profession and the public want, and should have, lawyers and judges who are of above average intelligence and learning. We believe—and experience shows—that a person must have demonstrated that he has sufficient intellect and drive to do more than barely pass college work before he should be admitted to the much more difficult and demanding work of the law school. This imposes no unreasonable burden on a student, for in our time anyone with intelligence and ambition can go to college, and have an opportunity to demonstrate his capabilities.

Everyone agrees that some minimum standards for entry into Law School need to be adopted. Disagreement comes over where to draw the line. And as Holmes once said, any line appears to be arbitrary when compared with that which lies immediately on either side of it. But a line there must be, if we are to have any standards at all.

It seems clear to those of us at the Law School who have studied the matter that our admissions standards now need adjusting, if for no other reason than to eliminate the human wastage we have been experiencing in recent years. Attrition during the first year of Law School has been thirty percent and more, composed about equally of voluntary withdrawals and academic failures.

This attrition represents an immense waste of time and of manpower for both students and faculty, a waste which the individuals and society can ill afford. It is actually unfair to a student to admit him to Law School when all the predictive factors available indicate that he will not pass the work. The best single predictive factor which we have is the student's undergraduate college academic record.

Experience now points quite clearly to the fact that a person who has done no more than the bare minimum acceptable work in college is very likely to fail in law school. Our accuracy of prediction is heightened when the national Law School Admission Test score is considered along with the college record.

We have an obligation to the applicants, to their parents, and to the good students to adjust our admissions standards so as to avoid a wasted year for those who are almost certain to fail. We are studying the matter closely with a view toward doing this for next year. In this move I earnestly solicit your backing.

When we do strengthen admissions standards, more people will be denied admission than in the past. I will certainly get more telephone calls and letters. But I ask you is it not better that a young person not invest time and money in an endeavor which is futile and frustrating for him and which dilutes the quality of education for the other students? Denials of admission do not seem to bother people until the case of a friend or relative comes along. This is understandable human nature. To the individual involved, and his family and friends, his case is always special. And we are entirely sympathetic to the human element, but when the Law School is confronted with this we are pressed back to the proposition that we either have standards or we don't. We never intend to be mechanistic or rigid, or to lose sight of the human concerns and the variety of factors bearing on a person's character and personality. But concrete experience shows that apart from other factors there is a certain academic and intellectual level which a person must have to be successful in the law school.

When the hard cases come, I hope we may have your understanding. You can be satisfied that before any application is denied the applicant receives the most careful consideration by a four-man faculty admissions committee and the committee's collective judgment governs. You may also be satisfied that we are acting in what we believe to be the best interests of the individual, the institution, the legal profession, and the public welfare.

I would ask of you the same understanding when a student who has been admitted is thereafter excluded for academic deficiency. Our job is to attempt to educate our students and to graduate them, not to fail them. Despite our best efforts, however, there will always be those who for one reason or another do not make the grade. For some, the law is simply not where their talent or interest really lies, and the sooner they discover this, the better. There are others whom the admissions process should have screened out initially but did not because of its imperfect nature. Then there are those who simply do not work or are not really interested. As our admissions standards are strengthened, our attrition rate will surely decrease.

While we do not want unreasonable standards, we do want an academic program which puts substantial demands on a student, one which taxes him and compels him to stretch his mind to its limit. The best legal education is conducted in an environment where the law completely absorbs the student's interest and inspires him to devote most of his waking hours to the law—to class work and to the other activities within the Law School and to reading in the vast literature of the law. To allow a student to limp through on a reduced or partial work load is a disservice to him and to the public. A life in the law, as you know all too well, is a demanding life, and one preparing for it should know that from the start. We are training tomorrow's leaders. A man can hardly be a winning mile runner if in training he never runs over half a mile. Nor can he bear the burden in the heat of the day if he is always allowed to work in the shade of the morning. We intend to turn out men with an intellectual toughness who can work hard and are dedicated to the best values of our legal tradition.

A Law School cannot wash its hands of all considerations of character and ethics among its students. We are not just another educational institution. We have a peculiar and indeed awesome public responsibility in matters of this sort. The Law School catalog now expressly provides that one of the requirements for the LL.B degree is that the student "have maintained, in the judgment of the faculty, a satisfactory record of honorable conduct befitting a prospective member of the legal profession." While the law faculty cannot and should not attempt to police all the private morals of our students, we cannot ignore conduct which involves moral turpitude or which goes to a student's basic honesty and integrity.

In this respect, the student-administered Honor System is our best hope. Happily, there is a resurgence of interest in the Honor System. Responsible, active students are a positive force in the educational climate of the school. A student committee is now studying the Honor System with a view to adopting revisions in the fall which will make it a more vital force in the life of the school.

There is a healthy rise in student activity all across the board, and in this is one of the most encouraging developments within the Law School.

This year students have activated a Law Forum to bring significant speakers to the school. One of the best programs was a debate between Maury Smith and an HEW attorney over the school guidelines.

Students have also recently inaugurated a Law School newspaper. This will do much toward building morale and will provide a means of keeping students and faculty informed of events and developments within the Law School. The paper is entitled the *Alabama Law Reporter*. Six issues are scheduled for publication next year. We contemplate that it will become a permanent feature of the Law School. The plan eventually is to put all active alumni on a mailing list to receive every issue, thereby providing you with news of the Law School at frequent intervals. It is possible that this may go into effect this fall.

A Student Legal Research Group is being planned. This organization will provide a research and memorandum-writing service for lawyers and judges everywhere, and it will provide excellent experience for the students. Problems can be sent in by mail, and the students will prepare memoranda under faculty supervision. Thus you will be able to tap readily the resources of our library as well as the analytical talents of our students, for a nominal cost. You will be informed when this group is activated.

One of the important services the Law School provides for the students and equally for the bench, bar, government agencies, corporations, and others is the Placement Service. The role of the Placement Service is to bring the prospective law graduate, and his interests, into contact with prospective employers, and vice versa. We view this as one of our most important services to you, and we want to do everything possible to make it efficient. Assistant Dean Guy Huthnance is in charge of placement, and he and I have laid plans for changes in the system, commencing this fall, which will provide better service to you.

Let me ask your cooperation on one matter which will make it possible for us to be of more help to you in placement. Times have changed. Very few students now come out of Law School with no place to go. Almost every law graduate has a choice of opportunities and is committed well ahead of graduation. Students graduating in May will often make commitments in the preceding fall, and most of them will have done so by February. Thus, if you are interested in obtaining a law graduate and if you are to have any range of choice, or any choice at all, you must think months ahead. We get numerous calls from law firms in May wanting a graduate to come with them the next month. We cannot often provide anyone that late in the year.

We welcome your inquiries about our students, and we will supply full data about them and will arrange interviews for you at the Law School. But I urge you to plan 6 to 8 months ahead so that we will have some wares to exhibit when you do inquire. The active placement season is generally fall and winter.

Nationally there is developing a pattern of summer law office employment of second-year law students. There is a mutual advantage here for the students and for the law firms. For a student, at the end of two years of law school, the two to three months experience with active lawyers is a valuable addition to his education, and it adds depth to his last year of Law School. For a law firm this arrangement provides some good assistance at relatively low cost for the summer and affords a way to look over a man for a possible permanent association in the future, but with no commitment.

Employing a second-year law student for the summer is a way in which every law office in the state can concretely participate in the Law School's educational program. Let me urge all of you to consider this for the summer of 1968, and every summer thereafter. As part of our placement service, we are planning to have information on all of our second-year students available in a systematic way, so that we can supply you with data and prospects. Please write us during the fall and winter if you can take a student next summer. I can assure you that the students themselves are keenly interested in this.

We are delighted to announce that the Law School is initiating a Defender Program in September. We have recently received a grant of $28,000 for the first year of the program from the National Defender Project. The director of the program is Professor Clinton McGee, assisted by Professor Sam Beatty. Law students will be assigned to work with a court-appointed counsel in criminal cases in state and federal courts in Tuscaloosa. New courses and seminars will be added to tie in the practical experience of the students to the curriculum. This program will enhance the educational experience of our students and will also provide a useful service to the bench and bar.

This program coincides with an expansion of our offerings in the criminal field as well as in other areas. This coming year we will have for the first time seminars in juvenile courts, in the sentencing process, and in current criminal law problems. We shall also be offering for the first time courses in admiralty and in corporate taxation, and seminars in the bill of rights, in problems of res judicata, and in constitutional litigation.

This past session a year-long course based on the Uniform Commercial Code was installed. Also offered for the first time last year were courses in Business Planning, Comparative Law, World

Peace and World Law, and Law and Psychiatry. All of these will be continued.

These new courses and seminars are in addition to the solid hard core of subjects which all of you may remember in Law School. The new offerings represent a broadening and a deepening of legal education and an effort to make the third year of Law School more responsive to the conditions of the world which the students will face.

This past spring we instituted a writing and research program for all first-year students. One of the constant complaints from the bench and bar is that law school graduates cannot write. This new program is an effort to begin remedying that deficiency in the very first year of Law School. We do not intend to drop it there. Starting this fall, all second-year students will be required to participate in a thorough-going, closely supervised appellate moot court program which will afford further training in research, analysis, writing, and oral communication.

The first year writing and research program, coupled with the second year moot court program, should give the student a good base from which he can further develop these skills in such activities as the student Legal Research Group, the voluntary moot court program, and the *Law Review*, all of which are being revamped and revitalized.

We had a stimulating and unique innovation this spring when Judge Seybourn Lynne held pre-trial conferences at the Law School. These were live unrehearsed conferences on the regular docket. The first-year procedure class attended. To my knowledge, this has not been done in any other Law School in our country.

Our curriculum expansion and the new programs for students we are offering all require a lot of faculty manpower—more than has been available in the past. We have been most fortunate in having generous University administration support in building the faculty. And we can take much pride in the new appointments we have made.

We will have five new young law teachers with us when school opens in September. These are all first-rate people who, so far as such matters can be judged, hold promise of being outstanding law faculty members. They come from five different law schools of real quality: University of Michigan, University of Chicago, Harvard, N.Y.U., and the University of Virginia. Their undergraduate college work was done at Amherst, Columbia, Vanderbilt, and the University of South Carolina. It is a great pleasure to be able to say that one of these new teachers is drawn from the practice of our own state bar, the president of the Young Lawyers Section of the Birmingham Bar—Vastine Stabler. When a young lawyer of this caliber chooses to leave the practice and join our faculty, it reinforces my faith that the Law School is really moving.

Among the critical ingredients in the faculty of a fine law school are good minds, imaginative scholarship, and stimulating teaching. I believe that these new recruits to our ranks will bring all of these qualities and add real academic strength to the enterprise.

In addition to these five men, two visiting professors from overseas will be with us. One is an Englishman, a Cambridge graduate who has been teaching law for some years at The London School of Economics. The other is an Australian, a graduate of Melbourne University, now teaching in the law school there. This past year we had three overseas visitors with us, and they were most successful. They do much for both faculty and students, and we hope to have one or more of them every year.

I could go on for some time telling you of things happening in the Law School. Despite the usual quota of headaches and frustrations encountered in the rapid development of an institution, we are clearly moving on all fronts, and moving in the right direction.

I must mention one financial statistic which dramatically illustrates this point. In the year 1965–66, the funds for law library books amounted to $30,000. This past year funds for books have come to $80,000. This is the result of enhanced University support and the Law School Foundation's efforts. The supplemental support we are getting and hope to get through the Foundation will mean the difference between success and failure in the development of the Law School. The report you will receive shortly will show that much has been done, and also that much remains to be done.

In this connection it is a pleasure for me to announce that Miss Katherine Farrah of Montevallo, the only child of Dean Farrah, is leaving in her will virtually her entire estate, which was Dean Farrah's estate, to the Law School Foundation, to establish the Albert J. Farrah Professorship.

Our neighboring state of Georgia provides a useful illustration of the possibilities. This spring Smythe Gambrell, of Atlanta, former president of the American Bar Association, gave $1 million to the Emory Law School. A year ago the Georgia Legislature appropriated $1 million for the law library at the University of Georgia. A group of Atlanta lawyers one of whom is Mr. John Sibley, has channeled several hundred thousand dollars to the University of Georgia Law School over the past three years. This is the kind of money it now takes for legal education, and this is the kind of money many law schools are now getting. I invite all of you to join with us, however small you feel your contribution may be, for collectively they add up to important amounts.

I continue to have faith that somewhere there is a Smythe Gambrell or a John Sibley who will recognize the importance of our Law School and will come to our aid in a massive way. And I refuse to believe that the legislators and public leaders in Georgia are more enlightened than ours, and more aware of what good legal education requires.

Surely no one can deny the critical importance of the Law School. The influence of educational institutions has been expressed in various ways in the past. The Duke of Wellington is supposed to have said that the Battle of Waterloo was won on the playing fields of Eton. On the afternoon of the Battle of Chancellorsville, Stonewall Jackson remarked to a group of officers, as the lines were forming up, "The Virginia Military Institute will be heard from today." I often think of that, for the University of Alabama Law School is heard from every day in hundreds of law offices, in dozens of courtrooms, in the public arena, in the legislative halls and executive councils of state and nation. The crucial role of this Law School as a training ground for our leadership can hardly be exaggerated. It is a supreme honor for all of us at the Law School to have the opportunity to contribute in this way to the future of society. I would like to express publicly my gratitude to the members of the law faculty who are working with enthusiasm and dedication to maintain and build a great Law School.

Farrah Hall was first occupied forty years ago this coming September. Perhaps some of you were there at the ceremony in which Dean Farrah accepted the keys to the building. I would like to close with a passage from his remarks on that occasion which still has a current ring:

> Our predecessors, with almost no accommodations and almost no equipment, have given to the State and nation many of its greatest lawyers and most useful public men. Therefore, with these greater advantages of building and equipment, the acceptance of this key imposes greater responsibilities upon present and future faculties and students of the Law School. In their name and stead, I solemnly promise that in so far as in my power lies, this structure shall not be a mere monument of brick and stone and steel to please the fancy of the casual passerby, but rather that it shall perform the great service to the State for which it was designed and thus become a veritable temple of learning, a shrine for real seekers after truth, a Mecca for those who would learn the law.

It is our great honor at the Law School today to renew that promise, and if our present momentum continues, men forty years from now will be able to look back and see that these promises have been kept.

Appendix D

Remarks of Dean Daniel J. Meador at Farrah Law Society Charter Members Dinner, Birmingham, Alabama, October 24, 1969

[After preliminary comments paying tribute to Heflin, Friend, and Pipes, and announcing the award of a charter in the Order of the Coif]

We have here two events within the past ten days—the award of the Coif charter and the overwhelming success of the Farrah Society membership drive—which together symbolize the progress of the recent past in pushing this Law School ahead to meet the needs of the late twentieth century. The two events are closely related, for without the great work of you here and many others we surely would never have been taken into Coif membership. We would have had no library development, no scholarship program, no faculty summer research grants or student assistantships, and little of student programs and visiting lecturers. You have supplied resources which, coupled with a gradually growing University budget, have enabled us to begin to do those things which a law school of real quality must do. We have achieved many of the immediate objectives which we set out to achieve over three years ago. Thus this week represents a landmark along the way in the development of the Law School, a marking of great progress thus far and a hopeful pointing to the future.

I view this evening as a kind of "family gathering." We are all here tonight because of our special interest in an enduring institution of great public importance—the University of Alabama Law School. Viewing this as a "family affair," I deem it appropriate to share with you a matter which I would not normally discuss on an occasion of this sort, for it involves me personally as well as the institution. But having worked with many of you in this common effort I feel that I should take the occasion to speak to you directly about this myself. I have always tried to deal with complete frankness and openness with persons interested in the Law School.

First let me state the matter and then offer a word of explanation. Next summer, after the close of this academic year, I will be leaving the Law School to accept the position of James Monroe Professor of Law at the University of Virginia.

I make this announcement with the greatest possible mixture of feelings. There is a deep sadness over the prospect of leaving Alabama and of ending the association with all of you which have meant so much to me personally and professionally over the past three and a half years. Those of you who know of my deep interest here will know that I have not taken this step lightly. Yet there is at the same time an enthusiasm over assuming a role which, in terms of law and professional work, I find more satisfying and rewarding.

To understand this decision you should know that when Dr. Rose approached me about the deanship here in 1966, I went through a wrenching mental experience. I loved the life of a law professor at Virginia. I had never aspired to be a dean. Nevertheless, I accepted the opportunity out of nothing less than a sense of duty, simply because this Law School and the State of Alabama were unique, and there was considerable evidence that something dramatic could be done to move the school ahead and to build rapidly toward a nationally recognized center of legal education and research. I have the deep satisfaction of knowing that we have moved far in that direction.

In modern times, deans, like university presidents, tend to be fairly short termers. And this is probably good. Events move so rapidly, ideas and changes come so thickly, that a frequent infusion of new blood is good for the institution. I felt from the beginning that I would not want to be a dean for life. But I was determined for a period of years to give this development effort every ounce of my energy and all the concentrated, around-the-clock thought of which I was capable, in order to help move us toward a rightful place in the legal and academic world, and to provide a higher quality training than ever before for Alabama's future leaders. In this I have tried to do my best often in difficult and frustrating circumstances. And in those circumstances it has always been those of you involved with the Foundation who have provided the hope and encouragement and support which is so badly needed.

When approached by Virginia in late summer, I was faced with an agonizing career decision. After many weeks of hard thought I finally came to the conclusion that this was something I should not decline. After all, the James Monroe Professorship is not available just every day, and the work of a law teacher is my first love.

The award of the Coif charter and the huge success of this Farrah Society have given me assurances of much accomplishment and they evidence a solid base on which those who come after can build further.

You may wonder why I am announcing this tonight. Having reached finally my decision some days ago, I felt that I wanted you, the best friends of the Law School, to hear of it directly from me before you learned it second-hand. This is the time of year in which decisions of this sort have to be made in the academic world. Having already discussed it with President Mathews, with the president of the Law School Foundation, and with the Chairman of the Farrah Law Society, I felt a public announcement could be delayed no longer. A search for a new dean should begin promptly. But I wanted the privilege of explaining it to you in person. I regret having to inject this note of a prospective farewell into an otherwise gala evening.

A brief word about the future. There is much yet to do, as you all know, the grand objective of a major law center should be pursued. If this is to be attained it will necessitate a vigorous continuation of our drive toward a true legal research library, the prompt addition of at least a half dozen or more new faculty members, and an uncompromising adherence to high academic standards in both student and faculty performance.

We have managed to arrange for an increasing number of our faculty to be involved in important state and national groups, such as the Association of American Law Schools, the National Defender Project, the Law School Admissions Test Council, the Commissioners on Uniform State Laws, and the Alabama Law Institute. Those involvements are of great value professionally to the individual faculty members and they bring added status to the school. They should be continued and expanded. There was far too little of this in the past.

The establishment of the Alabama Law Institute this fall is a step of immense importance to the future of law, government, and legal research. Based at the Law School, the Institute and the school can be of mutual value to each other. Fortunately, for the development of the Institute, Hugh Merrill, its first president, was able to prevail on Vastine Stabler of our law faculty to accept the position of director. Under his direction and with the firm backing of the Law School, the University, and the Bar, the Institute can contribute greatly to the improvement of the legal order. It is a key element of the projected law center. We at the Law School have supported the Institute enthusiastically since its inception and this should certainly continue.

You may be assured that I will continue to give my full and enthusiastic efforts for the remainder of this academic year to working with President David Mathews, with you, and all others to carry forward the Law School development. There is much that we can do. Let me say again, in closing, to every person who has worked for us and contributed in any way, that I am grateful to you beyond my power to express in words. I thank also the University officials for providing me with the opportunity, for a season, to be of some service to my native state in a cause that is not well understood but which is of incalculable importance.

The Law School needs your backing more than ever. Stay with it; insist that it have at all times the leadership and resources to make it a truly great institution in the service of society.

About the Author

Daniel John Meador is the James Monroe Professor of Law Emeritus at the University of Virginia. A native of Alabama, he attended The Citadel and was graduated from Auburn University and the University of Alabama Law School. He earned a Master of Laws degree from Harvard University. During the Korean War he served in the U.S. Army and was thereafter law clerk to Justice Hugo L. Black. After two years of law practice in Birmingham, he joined the law faculty at the University of Virginia, where he has spent most of his career.

Over the years his time at Virginia has been interrupted by other assignments, including service as dean of the University of Alabama Law School for four years, Fulbright Lecturer in England, IREX Fellow in the German Democratic Republic, and Assistant Attorney General of the United States. His major professional interest has been in the courts, state and federal, their procedure and jurisdiction. He is the author of numerous legal texts and articles and of three novels.

At the University of Virginia he received the Raven Award, Alumni Association Distinguished Professor Award, and the Thomas Jefferson Award. Other awards include the Justice Award from the American Judicature Society, Distinguished Service Award from the National Center for State Courts, Professionalism Award from the Virginia Bar Association, and awards from the American College of Trial Lawyers and the American Academy of Appellate Lawyers. He has served on numerous boards of directors, including the boards of the State Justice Institute, the American Society of Legal History, and the American Judicature Society. He is the founding president of the Cahaba Foundation, Inc.[65]

His wife, Jan, died in 2008. He has three children and seven grandchildren. He lives in Charlottesville, Virginia.